# Drug Therapy and Schizophrenia

# Psychiatric Disorders
## Drugs and Psychology for the Mind and Body

Drug Therapy and Adjustment Disorders

Drug Therapy and Anxiety Disorders

Drug Therapy and Cognitive Disorders

Drug Therapy and Childhood and Adolescent Disorders

Drug Therapy and Dissociative Disorders

Drug Therapy and Eating Disorders

Drug Therapy and Impulse Control Disorders

Drug Therapy for Mental Disorders Caused by a Medical Condition

Drug Therapy and Mood Disorders

Drug Therapy and Obsessive-Compulsive Disorder

Drug Therapy and Personality Disorders

Drug Therapy and Postpartum Disorders

Drug Therapy and Premenstrual Disorders

Drug Therapy and Psychosomatic Disorders

Drug Therapy and Schizophrenia

Drug Therapy and Sexual Disorders

Drug Therapy and Sleep Disorders

Drug Therapy and Substance-Related Disorders

The FDA and Psychiatric Drugs: How a Drug Is Approved

# Psychiatric Disorders:
# Drugs and Psychology
# for the Mind and Body

## Drug Therapy and Schizophrenia

## BY SHIRLEY BRINKERHOFF

MASON CREST PUBLISHERS
PHILADELPHIA

Mason Crest Publishers Inc.
370 Reed Road
Broomall, Pennsylvania 19008
(866) MCP-BOOK (toll free)

First printing
1 2 3 4 5 6 7 8 9 10
Brinkerhoff, Shirley.
Drug therapy and schizophrenia / by Shirley Brinkerhoff.
p. cm.—(Psychiatric disorders: drugs and psychology for the mind and body)
Summary: Describes the characteristics and drug treatment of schizophrenia, as
well as alternative treatments. Includes bibliographical references and index.
1. Schizophrenia—Juvenile literature. 2. Schizophrenia—Chemotherapy—Juvenile
literature. 3. Schizophrenia—Treatment—Juvenile literature. [1. Schizophrenia. 2.
Mental illness.] I. Title. II. Series.
RC514.B69 2004
616.89'82—dc21
2003004402

ISBN 1-59084-574-9
ISBN 1-59084-559-5 (series)

Design by Lori Holland.
Composition by Bytheway Publishing Services, Binghamton, New York.
Cover design by Benjamin Stewart.
Printed and bound in the Hashemite Kingdom of Jordan.

This book is meant to educate and should not be used as an
alternative to appropriate medical care. Its creators have made
every effort to ensure that the information presented is accurate—
but it is not intended to substitute for the help and services of
trained professionals.

Picture Credits:
Artville: pp. 50, 52, 99, 100, 114, 118. Autumn Libal: pp. 39, 58. Benjamin Stewart:
pp. 55, 70, 75. Comstock: p. 89. Corbis: pp. 12, 66, 106. Natiional Library of
Medicine: pp. 18. 81, 83, 84, 85. Photo Alto: p. 48. Photo Disc: pp. 20, 25, 26, 33, 57,
62, 64, 68, 76, 78, 92, 116, 123, 124. Rubberball: pp. 96, 109, 110, 112. Stockbyte: pp.
22, 30, 32, 35, 47, 102, 120. The individuals in these images are models, and the
images are for illustrative puposes only.

# CONTENTS

# INTRODUCTION

by Mary Ann Johnson

Teenagers have reason to be interested in psychiatric disorders and their treatment. Friends, family members, and even teens themselves may experience one of these disorders. Using scenarios adolescents will understand, this series explains various psychiatric disorders and the drugs that treat them.

Diagnosis and treatment of psychiatric disorders in children between six and eighteen years old are well studied and documented in the scientific journals. In 1998, Roberts and colleagues identified and reviewed fifty-two research studies that attempted to identify the overall prevalence of child and adolescent psychiatric disorders. Estimates of prevalence in this review ranged from one percent to nearly 51 percent. Various other studies have reported similar findings. Needless to say, many children and adolescents are suffering from psychiatric disorders and are in need of treatment.

Many children have more than one psychiatric disorder, which complicates their diagnoses and treatment plans. Psychiatric disorders often occur together. For instance, a person with a sleep disorder may also be depressed; a teenager with attention-deficit/hyperactivity disorder (ADHD) may also have a substance-use disorder. In psychiatry, we call this comorbidity. Much research addressing this issue has led to improved diagnosis and treatment.

The most common child and adolescent psychiatric disorders are anxiety disorders, depressive disorders, and ADHD. Sleep disorders, sexual disorders, eating disorders, substance-abuse disorders, and psychotic disorders are also quite common. This series has volumes that address each of these disorders.

Major depressive disorders have been the most commonly diagnosed mood disorders for children and adolescents. Researchers don't agree as to how common mania and bipolar disorder are in children. Some experts believe that manic episodes in children and adolescents are underdiagnosed. Many times, a mood disturbance may co-occur with another psychiatric disorder. For instance, children with ADHD may also be depressed. ADHD is just one psychiatric disorder that is a major health concern for children, adolescents, and adults. Studies of ADHD have reported prevalence rates among children that range from two to 12 percent.

Failure to understand or seek treatment for psychiatric disorders puts children and young adults at risk of developing substance-use disorders. For example, recent research indicates that those with ADHD who were treated with medication were 85 percent less likely to develop a substance-use disorder. Results like these emphasize the importance of timely diagnosis and treatment.

Early diagnosis and treatment may prevent these children from developing further psychological problems. Books like those in this series provide important information, a vital first step toward increased awareness of psychological disorders; knowledge and understanding can shed light on even the most difficult subject. These books should never, however, be viewed as a substitute for professional consultation. Psychiatric testing and an evaluation by a licensed professional are recommended to determine the needs of the child or adolescent and to establish an appropriate treatment plan.

# FOREWORD

by Donald Esherick

We live in a society filled with technology—from computers surfing the Internet to automobiles operating on gas and batteries. In the midst of this advanced society, diseases, illnesses, and medical conditions are treated and often cured with the administration of drugs, many of which were unknown thirty years ago. In the United States, we are fortunate to have an agency, the Food and Drug Administration (FDA), which monitors the development of new drugs and then determines whether the new drugs are safe and effective for use in human beings.

When a new drug is developed, a pharmaceutical company usually intends that drug to treat a single disease or family of diseases. The FDA reviews the company's research to determine if the drug is safe for use in the population at large and if it effectively treats the targeted illnesses. When the FDA finds that the drug is safe and effective, it approves the drug for treating that specific disease or condition. This is called the labeled indication.

During the routine use of the drug, the pharmaceutical company and physicians often observe that a drug treats other medical conditions besides what is indicated in the labeling. While the labeling will not include the treatment of the particular condition, a physician can still prescribe the drug to a patient with this disease. This is known as an unlabeled or off-label indication. This series contains information about both the labeled and off-label indications of psychiatric drugs.

I have reviewed the books in this series from the perspective of the pharmaceutical industry and the FDA, specifically focusing on the labeled indications, uses, and known side effects of these drugs. Further information can be found on the FDA's Web page (www.FDA.gov).

*A person with schizophrenia has a distorted and often frightening perception of reality. His speech and behavior may seem bizarre, and he often experiences delusions and hallucinations.*

# 1 | Defining the Disorder

When E. Fuller Torrey was a sophomore at Princeton more than forty years ago, he received a phone call with news that changed his life. The call was from his mother, in upstate New York, and the news she gave him was extremely disturbing. Torrey's younger sister, Rhoda, a high school senior, was lying in the front yard yelling, "The British are coming." Rhoda was attractive and intelligent, and there had been no warning that she would develop schizophrenia, a devastating brain disease.

Torrey went with his mother and sister to some of the best medical centers in America for help, but what they were told there made little sense. "At Massachusetts General, they said the schizophrenia had been brought on by the shock of my father's death when my sister was young," Torrey recalls. "It made no more sense to me than the man in the moon. Why didn't I have schizophrenia if that's what caused it?"

Torrey had known for years that he wanted to study medicine, but it was after the onset of his sister's schizophrenia that he decided to make psychiatry his specialty. So began a battle that has lasted for more than thirty years. Torrey has become the best-known schizophrenia researcher in the United States and a tireless, outspoken champion of patients with schizophrenia and their families.

In the 1970s, when the seriously mentally ill had no lobbying group to speak for them, Torrey helped build the National Alliance for the Mentally Ill (NAMI), which now has 170,000 members and has become a powerful political force.

Even though Torrey is a psychiatrist, he has had little patience with those in his profession who place the blame for schizophrenia on its victims. Well into the 1970s, many Freudian psychiatrists believed that the mothers of schizophrenics caused their children's schizophrenia. As late as the 1990s, Dr. Theodore Lidz was still publishing research on the link between bad parenting and schizophrenia. Commenting on this, Torrey wrote, "This book completes 45 years of pumpkin-headed research by Dr. Lidz."

In 1983, Torrey wrote *Surviving Schizophrenia: A Family Manual*, a book that has helped many families understand schizophrenia and provide a supportive, loving environment for family members who suffer from this disease. He donated the hardcover royalties from the book to NAMI— well over one hundred thousand dollars so far. Torrey has written many other books on mental illness, received the Special Friends Award from the National Alliance for the Mentally Ill, and has put together a team of researchers at Johns Hopkins University to conduct studies on possible viral causes of schizophrenia.

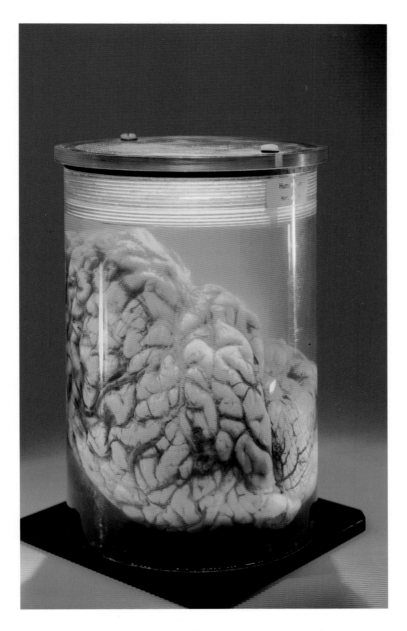

*Researchers use Torrey's collection of human brains to ex-
pand their knowledge of schizophrenia.*

**GLOSSARY**

*pathologists:* Specialists who study and diagnose the changes caused by disease in tissues and body fluids.

*atrophied:* Decreased in size or mass; wasted away.

One of Torrey's most important new ventures has been to develop a human brain bank from which he can provide brain specimens for researchers. Since 1994, he has built a network that collects brains of mentally ill people who died in their 20s, 30s, and 40s from suicide and heart failure, in car crashes and fires, and has even employed *pathologists* to hunt and collect these brains. Prior to this, the schizophrenic brains used for research were old and, in some cases, *atrophied*. Torrey's concern has been to get "better brains," those of younger people who had died recently, still full of unaltered proteins, neurotransmitters, and other compounds that might hold the answers to the cause of schizophrenia. The bank now holds more than two hundred brains, and many samples from these brains are sent to researchers worldwide free of charge. "Scientists historically have not shared their sources," says Dr. Stanley J. Watson, a professor from the University of Michigan who was provided with twenty thousand brain sections from Torrey's brain bank. "His attitude has been, the more horsepower, the faster we can all move ahead."

Torrey has created an internship program to help young scientists enter the field. He has also seen to it that about one hundred grants per year are distributed to researchers, a third of them to scientists outside the United States.

Torrey's interest in schizophrenia, sparked by his sister's disease, has never waned. He is still focused on finding a cure.

## AN INTRODUCTION TO SCHIZOPHRENIA

Schizophrenia is considered the most severe of the mental disorders, a disease with the potential to devastate not only the person diagnosed with it but in some cases that person's family as well. Schizophrenia is also a widespread problem, with one hundred thousand Americans newly diagnosed with the disease each year, at an annual cost to our society of ten to twenty billion dollars.

Because individuals with this disease suffer from disordered thought processes, they frequently become less able to communicate clearly and effectively. They may exhibit unusual speech and strange behaviors, and may *hallucinate* or have *delusions*. Such problems can lead to social isolation for those who suffer from schizophrenia, since people tend to avoid those who act in ways that seem strange, bizarre, or threatening.

Added to these difficulties is the debate about what causes schizophrenia, a debate that has gone on for decades without a conclusive answer. There was a time when many psychiatrists believed and taught that bad parenting—in particular, bad mothering—and other family problems were the cause of this disease. Because of this, much guilt and shame went along with the diagnosis of schizophrenia.

Now, however, opinions are changing. In *The New Psychiatry*, Dr. Jack M. Gorman writes:

> There is no question that schizophrenia is a severe brain disease caused by malfunction in one or more neurotransmitter systems in the central nervous system. No credible authority believes any longer that social circumstance, poverty, poor mothering, or willful behavior causes schizophrenia. . . . We are almost certain . . . that some cases are genetic while others are probably caused by environmental insults that disturb the developing brain during fetal life.

Gorman adds that research now indicates that the temporal lobe and the prefrontal cortex are the two areas of the brain that are most involved in schizophrenia and that the two neurotransmitters involved are dopamine and serotonin.

**G L O S S A R Y**

*hallucinate:* To have visions or imaginary perceptions.

*delusions:* A false belief based on a misinterpretation of reality.

(For more information about neurotransmitters, what they are, and how they work, see Chapter 4, "How Do Psychiatric Drugs Work?")

## SCHIZOPHRENIA IN HISTORY

The term "schizophrenia" is a relatively new one, coined in 1911. But how old is the disease itself? In ancient history, different forms of severe mental disorders were often recorded, sometimes under words like "madness," "insanity," or "lunacy." Torrey studied ancient accounts extensively and concluded that none of them actually indicate true schizophrenia. His study of mental disorders during the Middle Ages produced similar results. Although other mental disorders are described frequently in the literature from this period, it is not until 1656, when Georg Trosse, a minister in England, wrote about his own mental breakdown, that we find what Torrey calls "the first actual description in literature of what we now call schizophrenia."

> In his book *Surviving Schizophrenia*, Torrey writes:
>
> *The problems of blame and shame dwarf all others which arise between schizophrenics and their families. They lie constantly just beneath the surface, souring relations between family members and threatening to explode in a frenzy of finger-pointing, accusations, and recriminations.*

A few other accounts follow Trosse's, including those in the mid-1700s by Dr. Samuel Johnson, who believed that insanity was becoming more frequent in his time. Johnson attributed the increase in insanity to the fact that smoking was becoming less fashionable. Since smoking was believed to tranquilize the mind, Johnson reasoned that as smoking decreased, insanity would be more frequent.

---

## Treatment for the Mentally Ill in History

Individuals suffering from insanity were first gathered together into one place during the Middle Ages. First, they were put onto ships ("ships of fools") and sailed from port to port. Later, they were put into hospitals or asylums. In the thirteenth century, one of the first of these hospitals opened at Geel, Belgium, followed by similar facilities in Spain and England. Bethlem Hospital, the first hospital in England for this purpose, is where the term "bedlam," which means noisy confusion, originated.

---

Suddenly, in the early 1800s, the situation regarding schizophrenia seemed to change. At the same time, Philippe Pinel in France and John Haslam in England both wrote about cases of mental illness that appear to have been schizophrenia. Haslam's *Observations on Insanity* was first published in 1798, with a second edition appearing in 1809. The symptoms he described were clearly those of schizophrenia. Pinel's *Traite Medico-Philosophique sur l'Aliénation Mentale* was also published in 1809, and it, too, clearly described cases of schizophrenia. Pinel labeled the disease the *démence* syndrome, and that was the name that stuck until modern research began in the late 1800s. After these two men described schizophrenia, many more accounts followed, not only in medical writings but also in the general literature of the day, including Balzac's *Louis Lambert* (1812).

One idea was stated and restated throughout the nineteenth century—insanity was on the rise, echoing what Johnson had said earlier. By the 1800s, many people were discussing the situation with consternation. "The alarming increase of insanity . . . has incited many persons to an investigation of this disease," wrote Haslam in the preface to his 1809 book. "Insanity, in all its forms, prevails to a most

alarming extent in England . . . the numbers of the afflicted have become more than tripled during the last twenty years," wrote Sir Andrew Halliday in 1829. J. C. Prichard wrote, "The apparent increase is everywhere so striking that it leaves in the mind a strong suspicion that cases of insanity are far more numerous than formerly."

The rise of insanity was noted not only in England but in France, Denmark, Greece, Germany, Russia, Scotland, and Ireland as well, and observers agreed that this type of mental disorder was now appearing at younger ages. In 1856, Renaudin wrote that "Formerly insanity of early age was a very rare exception; now, on the contrary, we observe a marked *precocity* . . . it happens in all ranks of society and seems to be on the increase." This onset of insanity at an early age has a strong correlation with schizophrenia, which typically begins in the late teens and early twenties for males and between the mid-twenties and thirty for females.

> **GLOSSARY**
>
> *precocity:* Having mature qualities at an early age.

*This "asylum van" was used in a New Jersey town in the nineteenth century to transport people with mental illness. These people were perceived as being dangerous to society, so the windows were barred.*

The era of modern schizophrenia research began in the late 1800s, when psychiatrist Emil Kraepelin observed and identified this disorder as a kind of premature mental deterioration. He named it dementia praecox. In the early 1900s, Swiss psychiatrist Eugen Bleuler also studied the disease. He put together the two Greek words that mean "split mind" and came up with the term schizophrenia. Many people believe that "split mind" refers to split, or multiple, personalities, mistaking it for multiple personality disorder, one of the dissociative disorders. The mental splitting referred to in schizophrenia is the disorganization of mental processes, emotions, and behavior—a split from reality.

Bleuler did not agree with Kraepelin's earlier assessment that schizophrenia always began early in life and led to long-term deterioration. Instead, he identified four of the main features of schizophrenia, which came to be known as the four A's:

1. Disturbances of **affect** (emotion)
2. **Ambivalent** (simultaneously conflicting) feelings and attitudes
3. Irrational mental **associations**
4. **Autism**, or self-absorbed withdrawal

In 1911, the same year that dementia praecox was renamed schizophrenia, Sigmund Freud, the Austrian physician who founded psychoanalysis, published his ideas about psychoanalysis and mental illness. His psychoanalytic theory began to spread rapidly through the social sciences, literature, arts, and medical schools of America. Previously, people believed that schizophrenia indicated that something was amiss in the brain. Now, under the influence of Freud's ideas, the search for a cause turned toward psychosocial factors.

*Psychologists once attributed schizophrenia to problems in the mother-child relationship. Today, however, mothers are no longer blamed for this disorder.*

## Blaming the Victims

The old theory of the "Schizophrenogenic Mother" and other theories like it have caused a great deal of pain for families of patients with schizophrenia. In her book *This Stranger, My Son*, Louise Wilson describes how the pain and guilt affects parents in the following excerpts, which also reveal some of the prevailing ideas of that era about the causes of schizophrenia:

> Mother: "And so it is we who have made Tony what he is?"
> Psychiatrist: "Let me put it this way. Every child born, every mind, is a tabula rasa, an empty slate. What is written on it"—a stubby finger shot out, pointed at me—"You wrote there."

Wilson then writes about lying awake at night with these thoughts playing in her mind:

> We had moved too often during his early years. . . . My tension during the prenatal period when his father was overseas. . . . His father's preoccupation with his profession. . . . No strong companionship and father image. . . . A first child, and too many other children coming along too rapidly. . . . Our expectations were too high. . . . He had been robbed of his rightful babyhood, had grown up too fast. . . . Inconsistent handling. . . . Too permissive. . . . Too much discipline. . . . Oedipal fixation. . . .

## SCHIZOPHRENOGENIC MOTHER HYPOTHESIS

This early view attributed schizophrenia to the harmful influence of a cold and domineering mother, a view that is no longer considered valid in most cases of schizophrenia. Commenting on this theory, Gorman writes,

> Some psychologists concocted the particularly ridiculous notion of the "schizophrenogenic mother": an angry, con-

*According to Freud's way of thinking, a child might break with reality because of unconscious conflicts within him. Most modern psychology no longer ascribes to this way of thinking.*

trolling, and demanding woman who literally drives her children to psychotic behavior. . . . Sadly, blaming parents for causing schizophrenia was once a common phenomenon, leading to depressed, guilt-ridden people who not only had to watch their children suffer from a mysterious and sometimes devastating illness but who were also encouraged to believe they caused it. Fortunately, outstanding groups like the National Alliance for the Mentally Ill (NAMI) have cropped up in the last decade to enable families of people with schizophrenia to band together for their own defense and to advocate for patients with the illness.

## DOUBLE-BIND HYPOTHESIS

According to the double-bind hypothesis, patients with schizophrenia were victims of inconsistent, contradictory messages from family members. These messages were thought to cause so much stress in the patient that only total emotional escape could relieve it. Perrotto and Culkin give this example of a double-bind message in their book, *Exploring Abnormal Psychology*:

> A young schizophrenic man impulsively put his arm around his mother during her visit and she stiffened up, causing him to withdraw his arm. His mother then asked, "Don't you love me anymore?" and when he blushed, she said, "Dear, you must not be so easily embarrassed and afraid of your feelings."

## PERSONALITY

According to followers of Freud, schizophrenia was an attempt by the **ego** to break with reality since the patient was

**GLOSSARY**

**ego:** In psychoanalytic terms, the part of the mind that mediates between the person and reality.

thought to be in so much unconscious conflict that the only solution was to give up on the real world and resort to hallucinations and delusions.

Modern psychoanalysts have repudiated most of these theories. For one thing, little evidence supported them. Second, psychoanalysis and psychoanalytic psychotherapy have proven almost entirely useless in the treatment of schizophrenia. In fact, some patients with schizophrenia actually get worse during these therapies; the intensity of the self-scrutiny only make them more anxious.

## BIOLOGICAL CAUSES

Other theories about causes of schizophrenia include stressful events and the combination of social and cultural factors. However, most researchers in the field of schizophrenia now agree that the disease has a biological cause (or causes). This understanding grew out of studies begun in the 1940s that showed schizophrenia is an illness that is passed on in families genetically. While it is not proven that this is the only cause, the studies showed that patients with schizophrenia are far more likely to have family members with the disease than are people without schizophrenia. In fact, first-degree biological relatives of people with schizophrenia have a risk for the disease that is about ten times higher than that of the general population.

After determining this, researchers went on to study identical twins to see if the cause is in the genes or in the environment. Again, the evidence pointed toward genetic causes.

## THE SEARCH CONTINUES

However, even genetics does not tell the entire story. If the cause of schizophrenia was entirely genetic, then in all iden-

*A model of DNA, the building block of our genes. Scientists to-day believe that the reasons for schizophrenia are to be found here, in a person's genetic heritage.*

*Twin studies allow researchers to sort out the genetic and environmental causes of many diseases and psychiatric disorders.*

tical twinships where the disease occurs in one twin, the other twin should have it also. In the early 1990s, at the National Institute of Mental Health in Washington, D.C., Richard Suddath, Daniel Weinberger, and Fuller Torrey researched this issue. They found identical twinships in which only one twin had schizophrenia. By using magnetic resonance imaging (MRI), researchers could see that the twins with schizophrenia had brains that were slightly smaller than the brains of the other twins, particularly in the area of the brain called the temporal lobe, which controls emotions and memory. Researchers suggested that something had gone wrong during the development of the temporal lobe in those twins who developed schizophrenia.

Weinberger, a research chief at the National Institute of Mental Health, and his colleagues, researched the possibility that some insult to the brain during its development could cause schizophrenia. They damaged cells in the *hippocampus* of newborn rats and monkeys, and although the animals seemed relatively normal at first, they began showing abnormal behavior when they reached young adulthood, the time when late-developing parts of the brain that communicate with the hippocampus mature. This is a striking parallel to the development of human schizophrenia and has led to theories that the disease may be caused by damage to the brain while the infant is still in the womb. Such damage could come from a nutritional problem, an infection, or exposure to a toxin or virus.

## THE DOPAMINE HYPOTHESIS

Brain chemicals, particularly one called dopamine, are also involved in schizophrenia. Researchers first suspected that dopamine could be involved when they observed that pa-

**amphetamines:** *Drugs used to treat hyperactive children and symptoms of narcolepsy, as well as used as an appetite suppressant. Often abused as a central nervous system stimulant.*

**apathy:** *A lack of feeling, emotion, or interest.*

tients who took high doses of ***amphetamines*** (which cause a higher dopamine level) also exhibited schizophrenia-like symptoms. Too much dopamine activity appears to be involved in hallucinations, delusions, and thought disorder. Too little dopamine seems to be connected to withdrawal, ***apathy***, loss of pleasure, and decreased intellectual function. If patients with schizophrenia are given L-dopa, which the body can turn into dopamine, their condition often becomes worse. Because of these factors, and because the drugs that treat schizophrenia effectively are known to block dopamine, researchers suggested that too much dopamine may cause schizophrenia.

Researchers now understand that the dopamine hypothesis may be too simplistic. New medications such as clozapine (Clozaril) treat schizophrenia very effectively, but block far less dopamine than did the older drugs. These drugs have also been shown to block serotonin, another brain chemical that researchers now believe is also involved in schizophrenia.

In place of the older dopamine hypothesis, some researchers suggest that the positive symptoms of schizophrenia (delusions, hallucinations, disorganized speech, inappropriate affect, and disorganized behavior) result from too much dopamine activity in one area of the brain, while the negative symptoms (flat affect, lack of initiative, lack of conversation, and the inability to experience pleasure) result from too little dopamine activity in another area of the brain.

## SUMMARY

Schizophrenia is a puzzling disease, one that presents many questions to medical professionals and many problems to

Louise Wilson records this conversation with her son Tony:

"I read a book the other day," Tony said. "It was in the drugstore. I stood there and read it all the way through."

We waited, alarmed by the severity of his expression.

"It told what good parents ought to be. It said that people get . . . the way I am . . . because their parents weren't qualified to be parents."

"Oh Tony," I began, but Jack's signal silenced me.

"I'm a miserable wreck, because both of you are, too. You're queers and you never should have had a child."

"In what way are we queer?" Jack asked quietly.

"You never played ball with me. All you ever wanted to do was tramp around looking at birds or read. Or work in the . . . hospital."

"Well, maybe it would have been more fun for you if I'd been an athlete. I can see that. But I really don't see why that should make me such a terrible father."

"Read the book!" Tony exclaimed.

"Tony, there are a lot of things written in books, a lot of opinions that are inaccurate, distorted, or just plain wrong. Besides, I'm sure the book—"

"Listen, even the doctor that I've got here agrees! He says nobody's born with problems like mine!"

patients and their families. Now, though, there are psychiatric drugs available that can help many people diagnosed with schizophrenia to live more productive and fulfilling lives.

*A person with schizophrenia may appear listless and withdrawn from the rest of the world.*

# 2 | Symptoms of Schizophrenia

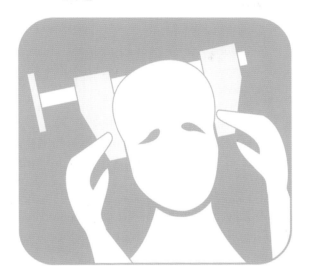

In *The Essential Guide to Psychiatric Drugs*, Jack M. Gorman presents the following three stories of how schizophrenia can begin and progress.

## PATTI

### Acute Paranoid Psychosis

Patti was an unremarkable child, the kind who neither excels at school nor gets into trouble. She was well liked by her teachers, had plenty of friends, and got along well with her brother. Her parents were very proud of her.

Once Patti graduated from high school and began classes at the local community college, however, she lost interest in her classes and had trouble getting out of bed in the morning. She grew listless and preoccupied. One evening, she threw a plate of food across the room, cursed, then ran outside. When she came back several hours later and her parents questioned her behavior, she shouted, "You will never take me alive."

Her behavior grew increasingly strange until the day she barricaded herself in her bedroom and screamed for hours, refusing to let anyone inside. When at last her father broke down the door, Patti was sitting on the floor, rocking back and forth, lighting matches.

At the hospital, she told the psychiatrist that she was being watched by "secret forces" who were putting thoughts in her head. She was given risperidone (Risperdal), which calmed her. Within two weeks, her symptoms went away, and she eventually returned to college. She continued taking Risperdal for several months before going off the drug.

## MARK

### Chronic Schizophrenia with Psychotic Symptoms Still Present

Mark was always shy and lonely as a child, often the scapegoat at school, physically awkward and clumsy. He did not make good grades, and at times he became interested in unusual subjects, like staring at pictures in a book of houseplants for hours on end.

In his early teens, Mark became disruptive in school, suddenly pushing another student without provocation, or laughing out loud for no apparent reason. He talked to his imaginary "friends" throughout the day, yet he frequently made little sense when he talked to real people. He showed little concern with personal hygiene, such as showering or brushing his teeth. He spent a large percentage of his time watching television and described the shows he had watched as if they were events that really took place.

Mark is now thirty and has seen many psychiatrists since he was sixteen. He has been tested many times and is

*Some people with schizophrenia may become angry for no apparent reason.*

*A person with one form of schizophrenia may show no expression at all; he never laughs, he never cries, and he speaks as little as possible.*

frequently admitted to hospitals, usually after sessions of pacing throughout the night, laughing and talking loudly to himself.

He has taken several different antipsychotic drugs, including Thorazine, Mellaril, and Stelazine. He also receives monthly injections of Haldol Decanoate, because he often forgets to take his medication orally.

Severely mentally disabled for life, Mark lives at home with his parents. If they die, however, Mark will probably have to be placed in an institution, since he does not have the ability to support himself.

## MARTY

### *Chronic Schizophrenia with Negative Symptoms*

Fifty-year-old Marty experienced his first symptoms of schizophrenia when he was twenty years old. In those thirty years, he has been hospitalized for the disease fifteen times. Marty has worked off and on throughout these years, sometimes delivering messages or sweeping floors in office buildings. He lives in a group home for patients with chronic schizophrenia.

Marty experienced both hallucinations and delusions earlier in his illness, but does not do so any longer. He has taken antipsychotic medications for most of the thirty years since his original diagnosis, but he is not taking them presently.

Although most of Marty's psychotic symptoms have subsided, he now has the negative symptoms of schizophrenia. He never laughs and he never cries. He does not look happy and he does not look sad. His face is expressionless. He moves slowly and talks as little as possible. When asked a question, he responds in short but appropriate answers.

## The Controversy Over Psychiatric Diagnosis

The idea of diagnosing people's problems is controversial. From a purely scientific perspective, critics have questioned the reliability and validity of a diagnostic system based more on expert consensus than on psychological measurement theory. From a humane standpoint, critics argue that diagnoses label people, not conditions. They consider the use of diagnosis to be dehumanizing because it applies a stigma that the person may carry for life and it may do nothing to help relieve the person's distress.

Those who defend the use of diagnosis say that diagnoses are formulated to label conditions, not people, and that they are useful in clinical research as well as practice. If we are to find effective therapies, we must be certain that we are evaluating the same type of problem from study to study. The use of strict diagnostic criteria helps ensure this. The use of diagnoses also helps clinicians make better predictions about how people will behave in future situations. We accomplish this by studying large numbers of people who have been diagnosed with the same disorder. Although resolution of these issues is awaited, psychiatric diagnosis remains influential in the field of abnormal psychology.

From Perrotto and Culkin, *Exploring Abnormal Psychology*.

He also suffers from tardive dyskinesia, a side effect of the antipsychotic drugs that causes him to make uncontrollable grimaces and chewing movements with his mouth.

Schizophrenia is a disease marked by psychotic symptoms, or symptoms that involve a "break with reality." The symptoms of schizophrenia can be divided into three categories: hallucinations, thought disorders, and delusions.

## HALLUCINATIONS

Hallucinations are false perceptions that have no basis in reality. In some cases, this may mean that the mind with schizophrenia distorts actual sensory input into something else. In the case of true hallucinations, however, the brain does not even need any other stimuli, but simply creates what it then hears, sees, feels, smells, and tastes.

Auditory hallucinations are the most common of the schizophrenic hallucinations. Onlookers may joke about a person "hearing voices," but to a patient with schizophrenia, the voices are as clearly heard as the voices of other human beings. Torrey reported one patient who for nearly seven years never had a single moment in which she did not hear voices, except during the hours she was asleep. Another patient heard voices continuously for twenty years, and they became louder when she tried to watch television. These hallucinations can sometimes provoke devastating behaviors, such as the murder committed by Joseph Kallinger, who reported hearing command hallucinations from "Charlie." Kallinger wrote a poem about these hallucinations:

(i cannot free myself from charlie)
bodiless rider, he rides thunderbolts in Hell
with the Devil sings doom songs
through his mouthless face
then comes to me with bloody instructions
(his favorite word is kill)

The voices individuals hear in hallucinations are usually negative, accusing the patient for past wrongs (real or unreal), and sometimes cursing them with language so vile the

patient hesitates to quote them to the therapist. On a few occasions, the voices may be kind or even helpful.

## THOUGHT DISORDERS

An individual's thoughts can be disordered in form—how he thinks—and in content—what he thinks. Formal thought disorder includes several abnormalities in form.

### Loose Associations

These are ideas that are disorganized or confused, which, when spoken, seem incoherent. This speech is sometimes called *word salad*.

### Clanging

This involves speaking in rhymes.

### Neologisms

This speech involves inventing words to express *idiosyncratic* thought.

In their book, *Exploring Abnormal Psychology*, Richard S. Perrotto and Joseph Culkin write that "Schizophrenic thinking often seems very irrational and defies the rules of logic, as in the statement "Jesus was a Jew; I'm a Jew; therefore, I'm Jesus." Impairment of abstract thought is also common among schizophrenics. For example, when asked to explain the saying "Strike while the iron is hot," the individual with schizophrenia may respond with a literal and concrete reply: "You have to hit something because you shouldn't need to iron so many clothes." One patient was asked the meaning of the saying "When it rains it pours," and replied, "Nothing more nor less than very wet weather."

*The human brain is like an old-fashioned switchboard opera-tor who receives and sorts all the incoming thoughts, emo-tions, and sensory input. In the brains of those with schizo-phrenia, the "operator" is no longer doing her job.*

GLOSSARY

*limbic: Relating to the parts of the brain that are concerned with emotion and memory.*

*synthesizes: Puts together parts or elements to form a whole.*

Torrey provides an apt description of thought disorder, followed by an actual patient's account of this experience. He writes that, in the normal human brain, probably in the *limbic* system, incoming stimuli are sorted and synthesized; then a correct response is selected and sent out. To illustrate this, he pictures a telephone operator sitting at an old plug-in type of switchboard in the middle of the limbic system, who receives and sorts all the thoughts, ideas, memories, emotions, and sensory input coming into our brains, then *synthesizes* the ones that go together.

However, in the brains of those with schizophrenia, the process no longer works the way it should—the "switchboard operator" appears to have decided not to do her job of sorting and synthesizing. When this happens, incoming stimuli no longer make sense. One patient could recognize the words other people were saying, but had to stop and figure out the meaning of each word. This meant that she couldn't comprehend sentences, because she was too busy deciphering the meaning of each individual word.

Here is one patient's description of how thought disorder feels:

I can't concentrate on television because I can't watch the screen and listen to what is being said at the same time. I can't seem to take in two things like this at the same time, especially when one of them means watching and the other means listening. On the other hand, I seem to be always taking in too much at one time and then I can't handle it and can't make sense of it.

I tried sitting in my apartment and reading; the words looked perfectly familiar, like old friends whose faces I remembered perfectly well but whose names I couldn't recall; I read one paragraph ten times, could make no sense of it whatever, and shut the book. I tried listening to the radio, but the sounds went through my head like a buzz saw. I walked carefully through traffic to a movie theater and sat through a movie which seemed to consist of a lot of people wandering around slowly and talking a great deal about something or other. I decided, finally, to spend my days sitting in the park watching the birds on the lake.

Torrey goes on to explain that response to stimuli is the job of this switchboard operator as well, noting that inappropriate responses are a hallmark of this disease. "For example," Torrey writes, "when told that a close friend has died, a schizophrenic may giggle. It is as if the switchboard operator not only gets bored and stops sorting and synthesizing but becomes actively malicious and begins hooking the incoming stimuli up to random, usually inappropriate, responses."

These inappropriate responses are at the heart of the patient's isolation and withdrawal. People whose behavior conforms to the norm as established by society find it extremely hard to communicate with those who respond in such unusual ways. People with schizophrenia, on the other hand, may find the whole understand-and-respond process so difficult that they withdraw and communicate with others as little as possible.

## DELUSIONS

Delusions are disorders in the content of an individual's thought, false beliefs held despite a lack of evidence. Trying to reason the individual out of their delusions is futile, like "trying to bail out the ocean with a bucket," says Torrey. He explains that, to the person experiencing delusions and hallucinations, they form part of a logical and coherent pattern. According to Torrey, if a person having delusions walked down the street and heard someone else on the street cough, he might take that cough as a signal of some

sort. If a helicopter then flew overhead, this too could become part of the "plot," and the person with delusions might decide the helicopter was observing him. If this person then gets to the bus stop too late to catch the bus, "obviously the person who coughed or the helicopter pilot radioed the bus driver to leave. It all fits together into a logical, coherent whole."

In some cases, the person having delusions is convinced that other people are controlling or manipulating her, and they are always looking for evidence to confirm their suspicions. Torrey gives as an example a patient of his:

> She believed that she had been wired by some mysterious foreign agents in her sleep and that through the wires her thoughts and actions could be controlled. In particular she pointed to the ceiling as the place from which the control took place. One morning I was dismayed to come onto the ward and discover workmen installing a new fire alarm system; wires were hanging down in all colors and in all directions. The lady looked at me, pointed to the ceiling, and just smiled; her delusions had been confirmed forever!

## OTHER SYMPTOMS OF SCHIZOPHRENIA

### *Grossly Disorganized Behavior*

Grossly disorganized behavior encompasses a wide variety of behaviors. It can include unpredictable agitation or childlike silliness; it may lead to difficulties in daily activities such as cooking a meal or keeping oneself clean. Some patients may dress in unusual ways, such as wearing several coats and scarves on a hot summer day, or may begin shouting and swearing without any provocation.

### Emotional Disturbances

Many people with schizophrenia show a lack of emotional responsiveness, called flat or blunted affect. This may show itself in inappropriate responses to tragic situations. For example, on being told that his mother had just died, a patient with schizophrenia might reply, "Okay, can I have a soda?"

Because the individual with schizophrenia is probably responding to internal, unrealistic stimuli rather than to the real stimuli around him, he may suddenly laugh out loud as though he had just heard a joke, or begin crying for no reason that is apparent to anyone else around him.

At times, those with schizophrenia show powerful emotions that change suddenly and unpredictably; these sudden changes are called emotional lability. At the other end of the emotional spectrum are apathy, an attitude of disinterest, lack of emotion, and listlessness. These are also typical symptoms of many schizophrenics.

### Altered Sense of Self

Individuals with schizophrenia not only experience distorted sensory perceptions; they sometimes also have impaired self-perceptions. They may experience inadequate ego boundaries, in which the distinctions they perceive between themselves, other people, and objects may be lessened. Or they may experience depersonalization, feelings of unreality about themselves.

## SCHIZOPHRENIA IN THE DSM-IV

*The Diagnostic and Statistical Manual,* fourth edition (DSM-IV), is the most recent classification of mental disorders by the American Psychiatric Association. This manual helps

mental health professionals make an accurate diagnosis of their patients. Accurate diagnoses are vital in selecting the most effective treatments and for predicting future events in patients' illnesses.

The DSM-IV classifies patients in terms of five factors, called axes. This multiaxial system involves first gathering as much information as possible about the patient, which leads to better treatment planning. These five axes are as follows:

1. the primary diagnosis, or the major problem the patient is experiencing
2. personality characteristics that are typical of the patient

*"Negative" symptoms of schizophrenia include a lack of facial expression and a "Who cares?" kind of attitude.*

3. relevant physical disorders
4. past stress to which the patient has been exposed
5. assessment of how the patient has functioned in the past

After the psychiatrist gathers information on each of the five axes above, he or she can then use the following information from the DSM-IV to determine if a patient actually has schizophrenia and, if so, what type:

Schizophrenia lasts for at least six months, a period that includes at least one month of active-phase symptoms showing at least two of the following behaviors:

- delusions
- hallucinations
- disorganized speech
- grossly disorganized or catatonic behavior
- negative symptoms

The symptoms of schizophrenia are divided into positive and negative categories. "Positive" in this case refers to the symptoms that show an excess or distortion of normal functions: delusions, hallucinations, and so on. "Negative" refers to diminished or loss of normal behavior, and includes apathy, social withdrawal, ***flat affect***, and poor attention.

> **GLOSSARY**
>
> ***flat affect:*** Not showing any emotion.

## SUBTYPES OF SCHIZOPHRENIA

Subtypes of schizophrenia are determined by which of the symptoms the patient exhibits at the time of her evaluation. Subtypes include paranoid, disorganized, catatonic, undifferentiated, and residual schizophrenia. According to the DSM-IV, the features of each subtype are as follows:

### Paranoid

- prominent delusions or auditory hallucinations
- delusions are **persecutory**, **grandiose**, or both
- other delusions with other themes may occur (examples: jealousy, religiosity, **somatization**)
- this subtype typically shows little impairment on cognitive testing, which may suggest that such patients will do better in their work and with independent living

### Disorganized

- disorganized speech, possibly including silliness and laughter unrelated to the speech content
- disorganized behavior (lack of goal orientation), which may disrupt daily activities such as showering, dressing, and preparing meals
- flat or inappropriate affect, which may also include grimacing, mannerisms, and other odd behaviors

### Catatonic

This is a **psychomotor** disturbance. It may involve immobility, excessive activity, extreme negativism (maintaining rigid posture against attempts to be moved), **mutism**, peculiarities of voluntary movement (assuming inappropriate or bizarre postures, or grimacing), **echolalia**, or **echopraxia**.

### Undifferentiated

This has characteristic symptoms of schizophrenia, both negative and/or positive, but does not meet the criteria for paranoid, disorganized, or catatonic type. It is a "catch-all" category for those patients who do not exactly match the other three categories.

### *Residual*

- a diagnosis used after at least one episode of schizophrenia, when a patient is currently without prominent positive symptoms
- continuing evidence of the disturbance continues, indicated by negative symptoms and two or more other symptoms.

## PREDICTING THE OUTCOME OF SCHIZOPHRENIA

There is a widespread idea that those who "get" schizophrenia never recover, but this is not correct. Many such people recover and regain most of their mental functioning.

*A person with disorganized schizophrenia may grimace and make odd gestures for no apparent reason. The same symptoms, however, may be caused by tardive dyskinesia, a side effect of some psychiatric drugs.*

*Age of onset is just one factor that affects the outcome of schizophrenia.*

This fact has led to investigation by researchers about which patients might have a good outcome (recovery) and which are less likely to have such a positive outcome. According to Torrey, in *Surviving Schizophrenia, a Family Manual,* the following factors are included in determining possible outcome (though he cautions that these are only statistical assertions of likelihood and must be taken together, not as individual signs).

### History Prior to Onset of Illness

Patients who were thought to be relatively normal prior to getting sick were more likely to have a good outcome. If, on the other hand, these patients were always considered "strange" by others, had serious problems with people in their age group or at school, or were very withdrawn, they were more likely to have a negative outcome.

### Family History

Patients whose families have no other members with schizophrenia have the best outcomes. The more close relatives who have schizophrenia, the poorer the outcome tends to be. However, a history of depression or *manic-depressive* (or bipolar) illness among close family members does not seem to affect the patient's outcome negatively.

### Age

Patients whose schizophrenia develops at a younger age tend to have poorer outcomes. For example, those who experience onset of the disease before the age of fifteen are likely to have a less positive outcome than those with onset at twenty-five, who in turn have a less positive outcome than those with onset at thirty.

**GLOSSARY**

**manic-depressive:** Bipolar disorder. A mood disorder characterized by periods of extreme elation and energy with periods of extreme sadness and loss of interest in activities.

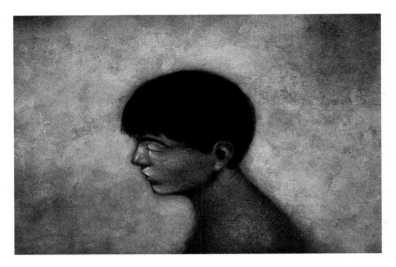

*A person with schizophrenia who is catatonic, has flattened or absent emotions, or is depressed is less likely to have a positive outcome to his disorder.*

### Suddenness of Onset

Those who have the most sudden onset of schizophrenia typically have the best outcome.

### Prior Events

Precipitating events are a less dependable predictor of outcome, in part because those in the usual age of onset (fifteen to twenty-five) are in a period of much change. However, if major life events have preceded the schizophrenic breakdown, this signals a great likelihood of a good outcome.

### Symptoms

Some symptoms seem to indicate a greater likelihood of a good outcome. These include catatonic and paranoid symptoms and depression. Flattened or absent emotions are more likely to signal a poor outcome, as are withdrawal, apathy, indifference, or a marked thinking disorder.

In a final word on predicting the outcome of this disease, Torrey notes that he has seen patients who have all or most of the predictors that point toward a positive outcome who never recover and whose outcome is, in actuality, poor. "More optimistically," he writes, "I have seen patients with virtually every poor prognostic sign go on to almost complete recovery."

## SUMMARY

Schizophrenia begins in various ways and runs a different course with each patient. This can make diagnosing and treating schizophrenia a difficult and challenging task. However, dedicated health care professionals and researchers continue to work to make both the diagnosis and treatment of schizophrenia more efficient and successful.

*People with schizophrenia often live in a frightening world of hallucinations.*

# 3 | History of the Drugs

One of the most brilliant men in the field of mathematics is John Nash. He was awarded the 1994 Nobel Prize in Economic Science (jointly with Harsanyi and Selten) for his work on game theory.

Nash has also had schizophrenia.

From the early years of his life, Nash showed unusual personality characteristics, including a lack of interest in other children. Born in 1928 in Bluefield, West Virginia, Nash was brought up in a loving family that included a younger sister. There were also cousins living nearby. Nash, however, preferred to play alone with his toy airplanes and Matchbox cars.

Nash's parents encouraged his education, making sure he had good instruction and science books to read. By the age of twelve, Nash was frequently performing scientific experiments at home. Nash's teachers were less aware of his extraordinary talents than they were of his lack of social skills, and labeled him "backward."

## How Prevalent Is Schizophrenia?

*"There are as many schizophrenics in America as there are people in Oregon, Mississippi and Kansas, or in Wyoming, Vermont, Delaware and Hawaii combined."*
—President's Commission on Mental Health, 1978

According to Dr. E. Fuller Torrey, schizophrenia strikes nearly one out of every one hundred Americans at some time. The disease is twice as common in Scandinavia, and in western Ireland it affects an estimated one of every twenty-five people. When his book *Surviving Schizophrenia, a Family Manual* was written in 1983, Torrey estimated that "on any given day there are 600,000 people with schizophrenia under active treatment and each year another 100,000 Americans are diagnosed with it for the first time."

Other experts estimate that about 1.8 million people in the United States have schizophrenia, and that race, gender, and culture do not affect who gets it and who does not. Schizophrenia most commonly begins between the ages of sixteen and twenty-five for males, and twenty-five and thirty for females, although it can begin at older ages. Women usually are not affected as severely as men and are able to function better in their community even while experiencing schizophrenia.

Nash entered Bluefield College in 1941 and pursued not only chemistry, a favorite interest of his, but also mathematics. At this time, his unusual abilities in math were beginning to show, but he behaved in an eccentric way and had few friends. He later won a scholarship and entered Carnegie Institute of Technology (now Carnegie-Mellon University) in 1945, where his growing interest in math led him to take more and more courses in this field.

By 1952, Nash was teaching at the Massachusetts Institute of Technology. His research in several areas of higher mathematics was seen as a very significant contribution to the field. During his time at MIT, however, Nash began experiencing symptoms of mental illness, though at first these symptoms were not recognized for what they were.

He exhibited bizarre behavior, such as at the 1959 New Year's Eve party when Nash reportedly arrived dressed in odd and inappropriate clothes. He spent most of the evening curled up on his wife's lap.

When he began teaching his game theory course on January 4, 1960, his opening comment to the class was, "The question occurs to me. Why are you here?" Nash handed his course over to a graduate student and vanished for a few weeks. It is said that, when he returned, he walked into the common room with a copy of the *New York Times,* saying that it contained encrypted messages from outer space that

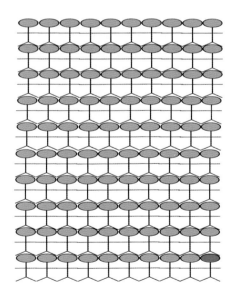

*According to Dr. Torrey's research, one out of a hundred Americans will experience schizophrenia sometime in their lives.*

## Brand Names vs. Generic Names

Talking about psychiatric drugs can be confusing, because every drug has at least two names: its "generic name" and the "brand name" that the pharmaceutical company uses to market the drug. Generic names come from the drugs' chemical structures, while brand names are used by drug companies in order to inspire consumers' recognition and loyalty for their products.

Here are both the brand names and generic names for some of the psychiatric drugs mentioned in this book:

Ativan® (lorazepam)

Clozaril® (clozapine)

Depakote® (valproate)

Haldol® (haloperidol)

Mellaril® (thioridazine)

Navane® (thiothixene)

Paxil® (paroxetine)

Prolixin® (fluphenazine)

Prozac® (fluoxetine)

Risperdal® (risperidone)

Seroquel® (quetiapine)

Stelazine® (trifluoperazine)

Thorazine® (chlorpromazine)

Tofranil® (imipramine)

Trilafon® (perphenazine)

Valium® (diazepam)

Xanax® (alprazolam)

Zoloft® (sertraline)

Zyprexa® (olanzapine)

were meant only for him. At first, people around him who were accustomed to his unusual behavior considered it all a joke. However, after months of bizarre behavior, his wife had Nash hospitalized at McLean Hospital, a private psychiatric hospital outside of Boston. When he was released, he resigned from his position at MIT, withdrew his pension, and traveled to Europe, intending to renounce his United States citizenship. His wife followed him and had him deported back to the United States. Back in the United States, Nash's illness went on, and he spent the majority of his time on the campus of Princeton University, talking about himself in the third person as Johann Von Nassau, writing nonsensical postcards, and making phone calls to former colleagues.

In 1961, Nash's mother, sister, and wife committed him to New Jersey's Trenton State Hospital, and an extended period of treatment, recovery, and further treatment followed. His wife divorced him in 1962. Nash appeared to be "lost to the world," removed from ordinary society, although he spent much of his time in the mathematics department at Princeton.

Nash himself later wrote that he felt "the staff at my university, the Massachusetts Institute of Technology, and later all of Boston were behaving strangely towards me. . . . I started to see crypto-communists everywhere. . . . I started to think I was a man of great religious importance, and to

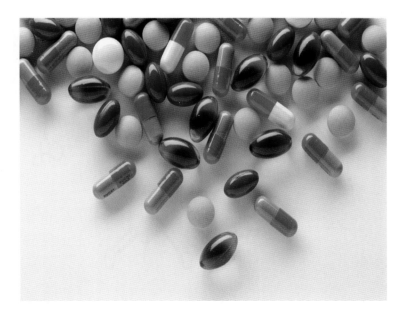

*Each drug has two names—its generic name and its brand name.*

hear voices all the time. I began to hear something like telephone calls in my head, from people opposed to my ideas. . . . The delirium was like a dream from which I seemed never to awake."

Nash began recovering from schizophrenia in the 1990s. He has continued to experience success in his mathematical work throughout his life, even though he was forced to spend periods of time in the hospital because of his mental condition.

Today, if someone were to experience the same psychiatric difficulties that Nash did, his physician's first step after diagnosis would be to begin him on a ***regimen*** of psychiatric drugs.

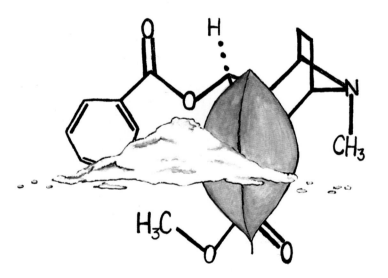

*A coca leaf and its chemical diagram. Coca is used to make cocaine, an illegal substance today, but a hundred years ago doctors prescribed it as an antidepressant.*

## PSYCHIATRIC DRUGS IN HISTORY

It has been a common practice for thousands of years of human history to use drugs that alter the mental state. Some of the drugs commonly used for this purpose include alcohol, *opiates*, cocaine, and *peyote*. It is thought that these drugs change behavior by acting on brain systems that govern behaviors such as sleeping, eating, and sexual behavior. Prior to the twentieth century, people could see the effects of such drugs but had little or no idea of how these effects were produced. In modern times, however, researchers and medical health professionals who study the brain are gaining more and more insight into how psychiatric drugs operate.

Ayurmedic texts of India from over two thousand years ago refer to a medicine made from the Rauwolfia serpentina plant. According to Bruce M. Cohen in *Mind and Medicine, Drug Treatments for Psychiatric Illnesses*, this medicine was used to treat symptoms similar to those of schizophrenia and *bipolar* disorder, though it was not understood how the drug worked. In the 1930s, reserpine, which was probably the active ingredient in this ancient medicine, was isolated and studied. Reserpine was then used to effectively treat psychotic disorders during the 1950s.

Another example is lithium, a drug often prescribed today for individuals with bipolar disorders. Writings from the time of the Roman Empire recommended that patients with *mania* use water from specific alkaline springs, water that is now thought to have contained lithium.

Plant preparations that contain opium have been used in the treatment of pain for hundreds of years. In the last two centuries, derivatives of these plants were used to treat psychic disorders and depressions.

Coca leaves, the source of cocaine, were used more than a hundred years ago as a stimulant and antidepressant. Sigmund Freud was one of the individuals who chewed coca leaves.

## MODERN PSYCHIATRIC DRUGS

Between the beginning and the middle of the twentieth century, severe mental illness in America grew to such an extent that people institutionalized in mental hospitals increased from two out of a thousand to four out of a thousand. There was little treatment available for such patients, however, and they often were simply shut away in state institutions. The most popular psychiatric treatments at the time were electric shock or various psychotherapies.

The treatment of many psychiatric ailments was about to change dramatically, however, with the discovery and development of new drugs that altered mood, behavior, and mental functioning. Help would soon be available for mental disorders that were considered untreatable just a few decades before.

Henri Laborit, a surgeon in Paris, was responsible for discovering one of the earliest known psychiatric drugs. Interestingly enough, that drug, chlorpromazine hydrochloride (Thorazine), was already in use as an antihistamine. Laborit had been puzzling over the problem of reducing surgical shock in his patients when, in 1952, he discovered that if he gave his patients a strong dose of antihistamines prior to surgery, they became much less anxious about the surgery. This decrease in anxiety levels allowed Laborit to sedate his patients with less anesthetic, which produced the exact effect he had been searching for—it reduced surgical shock among his patients. Laborit did not stop there, however.

When he saw how chlorpromazine affected the mental state of his patients, Laborit began to visualize another use for this drug—in the field of psychiatry. When psychiatrist Pierre Deniker tried chlorpromazine with his most agitated and uncontrollable patients, the results were amazing. Patients who had needed to be restrained because their behavior was violent could now be left unsupervised. Patients immobilized by catatonic schizophrenia could now respond to other people. It was a long and difficult struggle to get medical professionals to treat mental disorders with a drug, but eventually some began to try chlorpromazine in state institutions. Once again, the results amazed observers.

## Drug Approval

Before a drug can be marketed in the United States, it must be officially approved by the Food and Drug Administration (FDA). Today's FDA is the primary consumer protection agency in the United States. Operating under the authority given it by the government, and guided by laws established throughout the twentieth century, the FDA has established a rigorous drug approval process that verifies the safety, effectiveness, and accuracy of labeling for any drug marketed in the United States.

While the United States has the FDA for the approval and regulation of drugs and medical devices, Canada has a similar organization called the Therapeutic Product Directorate (TPD). The TPD is a division of Health Canada, the Canadian government department of health. The TPD regulates drugs, medical devices, disinfectants, and sanitizers with disinfectant claims. Some of the things that the TPD monitors are quality, effectiveness, and safety. Just as the FDA must approve new drugs in the United States, the TPD must approve new drugs in Canada before those drugs can enter the market.

Chlorpromazine was approved by the U.S. Food and Drug Administration in 1954 and had a great effect on patients with mental disorders, decreasing the intensity of schizophrenia symptoms such as hallucinations and delusions. It calmed people without sedating them and, in many cases, allowed them to lead an almost normal life. By 1964, fifty million people around the world had taken the drug.

This was only the beginning of the development of psychiatric drugs. One of the side effects associated with chlorpromazine was to produce symptoms similar to those of Parkinson's disease. Researchers reasoned that, if a chemical substance such as this drug could produce effects that mimicked those of Parkinson's, perhaps similar chemicals found in the brain could be causing actual Parkinson's disease. They began studying how they might counteract these chemicals. This new way of thinking about chemicals in the brain eventually resulted in understanding the role of dopamine and other neurotransmitters, an advance that has had great impact on the treatment of mental disorders. (An explanation of how neurotransmitters work in the central nervous system can be found in chapter four.)

Eventually, researchers discovered that antipsychotics such as chlorpromazine relieved hallucinations and delusions by blocking dopamine receptors in the brain. As a result of this discovery, scientists began exploring the possibility that schizophrenia could be caused by an excess of dopamine.

Later, using these same principles, researchers discovered the relationship between depression and a lack of the neurotransmitters serotonin and noradrenaline. On the same basis, they investigated whether or not anxiety could be caused by a lack of GABA (gamma-aminobutyric acid, another neurotransmitter).

More and more psychiatric drugs were developed because of this new understanding of how medications affect

*Researchers today are continuing to look for new ways to chemically treat psychiatric disorders.*

*Today, many psychiatric drugs are available.*

the brain. After chlorpromazine, other antipsychotics were developed, including the new atypical antipsychotics that have fewer side effects.

Other classes of drugs followed, targeting different mental disorders. The benzodiazepines, such as Valium and Xanax, were developed in the late 1950s and were used effectively in treating anxiety. Unfortunately, their use is limited by their potential to be addictive and by their many side effects. Research continued for drugs that could produce the same positive effects without the drawbacks.

One class of antidepressant drugs, the monoamine oxidase inhibitors (MAOIs), was discovered in the course of tuberculosis (TB) treatment. Some patients with tuberculosis also suffered from depression. When these patients were given an antibiotic called iproniazide for their TB, they also experienced relief from their depression. Iproniazide also helped alleviate patients' problems with appetite, energy, and sleep. Investigative studies showed that iproniazide produced its effects by inhibiting an enzyme called mono-amine oxidase. This set in motion a process that led to a higher concentration of neurotransmitters called the mono-amines (norepinephrine, serotonin, and dopamine) in the brain, thus helping relieve depression. (See chapter four for more details on how different classes of drugs work.) This led to the development of more MAOIs.

The last half of the twentieth century also saw the advent of two new types of antidepressants—the tricyclic anti-depressants (TCAs) and the selective serotonin reuptake inhibitors (SSRIs). The TCAs were discovered while re-searchers were looking for other antipsychotics. They no-ticed that one of the compounds they tested seemed to sub-stantially help depressed patients. This compound was named imipramine HCl (Tofranil). This highly successful antidepressant drug, which became the first of the TCAs, is still used today. In the 1980s, pharmaceutical companies began searching for another class of drugs that would have fewer side effects than the TCAs. The new class of drugs they designed, the SSRIs, blocked the reuptake of serotonin, but not norepinephrine. The first of these drugs was called fluoxetine HCl (Prozac). It was followed by several others, including sertraline HCl (Zoloft) and paroxetine HCl (Paxil).

## OTHER MEDICAL ADVANCES

The medical advances of the last few decades have come not only in discovering and developing new psychiatric medica-tions but in genetic research as well. Some psychiatric dis-eases, such as schizophrenia and bipolar disorder, have now been linked at least in part to abnormal genes, and re-searchers hope that this discovery will provide new ways to treat these diseases.

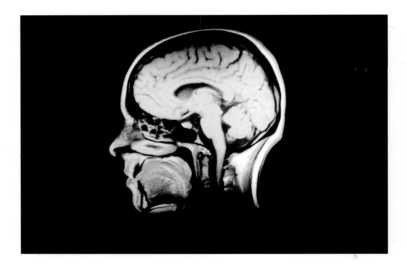

*MRIs allow researchers to see the details of brain structure.*

At the same time, researchers have developed methods to study psychotherapies under controlled conditions. Now psychotherapy and drug therapy can be compared scientifically, allowing practitioners to gain a better understanding of the uses and limitations of both types of treatment.

## BRAIN-IMAGING TECHNIQUES

Understanding how psychiatric drugs work inside the brain helps medical professionals know which medications to prescribe for which disorder. It also provides researchers with important information for developing new drugs. Imaging techniques developed in the last few decades have made this information more readily available, solving some of the difficulties in seeing inside the human brain.

With most other body organs, a simple blood test can provide vital information about that organ. Information about the brain is harder to come by. Many medicines are unable to get into the brain because of what scientists refer to as the ***blood–brain barrier***.

Now, however, researchers can inject chemicals labeled with tiny amounts of radioactivity into a person's bloodstream. They can then study where the chemicals go inside the brain, and to what receptors they bind. The most commonly used imaging techniques include:

- CAT (computerized axial tomography) scans reveal brain structures without harming the patient.
- MRI (magnetic resonance imaging) gives highly refined pictures of the brain using magnetic fields without using radiation.
- PET (positron emission tomography) and SPECT (single-photon emission computed tomography) reveal brain structure and also show metabolic activity in various parts of the brain (brain chemicals and their receptors).

### GLOSSARY

***blood–brain barrier:*** *The boundary created by the walls of the brain capillaries that prevents most proteins and drugs from passing from the blood into the brain tissue and cerebrospinal fluid.*

## SUMMARY

Many of the psychiatric drugs now in use have been developed as a result of observation on the part of medical professionals who noted positive results (in addition to the results they expected) when administering these drugs. Research in this field continues, with new drugs being developed and tested on an ongoing basis.

*The manufacture of psychiatric drugs is based on years of scientific research.*

# 4 | How Do Psychiatric Drugs Work?

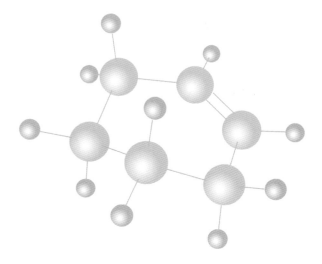

Peter Green, cofounder and former guitarist for Fleetwood Mac, lived through drug-induced schizophrenia.

By 1969, Fleetwood Mac had a string of hits, including "Black Magic Woman" and "Man of the World." It was voted Britain's best band by readers of the weekly *New Musical Express*. By May of 1970, however, Peter Green had left the band.

"It was a freedom thing," Green says. "I wanted to go and live on a commune in Germany. In the end I never did, but I had to get away. Acid had a lot to do with it."

Acid, or LSD, was one of the drugs that led Green into a condition that would eventually be diagnosed as schizophrenia. Green, who was once one of the most famous guitarists in British rock, stopped making music and gave away his guitars. He was committed to a hospital after becoming violent, and in his own words, "throwing things around and smashing things up."

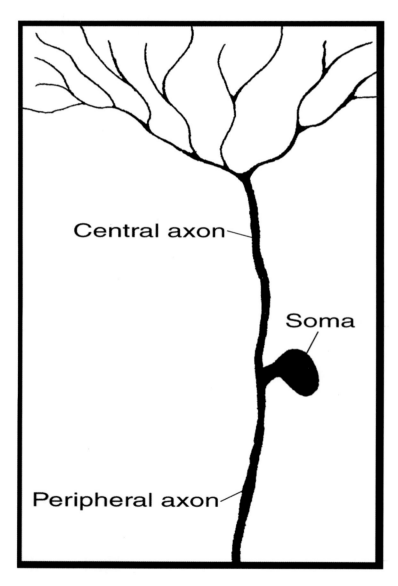

*Part of the structure of a nerve cell.*

At the hospital, Green was treated with tranquilizers, which made it a struggle to simply stay awake. "You don't know what you are doing," he says of that time. "You don't feel alive." Green was taking seventeen pills a day, and one friend comments that he would stand for hours in the garden with her, not saying a word.

Eventually, Green decided to stop taking his medication. Although he still heard voices from time to time, he began playing guitar again and even formed another band. Today, according to the Schizophrenia Homepage, Green lives with friends in southern England who have "helped him inch his way back toward normalcy. His behavior is no longer frightening, although he remains endearingly eccentric."

The complicated function of our brains can be disrupted by substance abuse, as happened with Peter Green. Other factors, caused both by genetics and environment, can have the same effect. The brain has long been a mystery and a source of amazement. Researchers have worked for decades to uncover how the brain works, and although we now have a partial picture, there is still much to learn.

Psychiatric drugs that are used to treat schizophrenia do their work inside the brain. Drugs and medications can change the patterns of firing in neural circuits; they can affect brain activity. By doing so, they can alter the aspects of consciousness that make us most human. A basic understanding of how the brain operates is necessary to understand how psychiatric medications can help in the treatment of schizophrenia and other mental disorders.

The brain is made up of many millions of neurons, or highly specialized cells that pass messages between them. Neurons are not found only in the brain. The central nervous system (CNS), which includes the spinal cord, also contain neurons, both sensory and motor. Our five

senses—sight, hearing, smell, touch, and taste—feed information from the outside world to the brain by way of these sensory neurons. Motor neurons then respond to this information by making the muscles of our bodies move.

Our motor and sensory neurons work together to move us out of harm's way whenever we face danger or feel pain. For instance, if we reach into a microwave to take out a freshly baked potato that is still too hot to touch, our sensory neurons relay that information from neuron to neuron until it reaches our spinal cord. There, information is sent back to our fingers on the hot potato, telling them to move out of harm's way. All of this happens in the blink of an eye or less, while at the same time information about the dangers of touching hot baked potatoes is being stored in our memory so that we will exercise caution the next time we reach for one.

Neurons have a special design that enables them to carry messages efficiently. Each neuron has a cell body, and from that center, it sends out dendrites and axons. Dendrites are projections that look like tiny twigs. Axons are long, thin filaments, with several terminal buttons at the end. The terminal buttons lie on the dendrites of other neurons, so that each neuron functions as a link in the communication chain. This is not a chain that runs in only one direction, however. Each neuron is in contact with many other neurons, making the CNS into a vast mesh or web of interconnected groups of neurons. All of the possible communication interconnections between these millions of neurons—with their cell bodies, axons, and dendrites—make up the human body's information superhighway.

Brain cells communicate by sending electrical signals from neuron to neuron. While the axons and dendrites lie very close together, they do not actually touch other neu-

## Types of Delusional Beliefs

*Grandeur:* believing you have magical or extraordinary abilities. For instance, an individual may believe that he has been chosen by God to save the world from nuclear disaster.

*Identification:* believing you are a well-known historical or present-day figure, such as Winston Churchill, Napoleon, or a famous movie star.

*Persecution:* thinking that other people want to harm you. An example would be a person who is convinced that her landlord is putting chemicals into her water in order to poison her.

*Reference:* thinking that world events and the behaviors of other people some-how relate to you. A person with this problem may feel that strangers laughing in a public restaurant are mocking him.

*Sin or guilt:* believing you are responsible for tragedies that take place, such as feeling guilty because you think a plane crash is your fault.

*Thought broadcasting:* thinking that you can send your thoughts into other people's minds. For example, a person in a subway station may believe he can control other people around him by sending them mental commands.

*Thought insertion:* believing that other people are putting thoughts into your mind. For instance, a person may believe that terrorists are using radio signals to send violent fantasies into her mind.

rons. In between is a tiny space called a synapse. Nerve impulses travel through this synapse, jumping the space in much the same way an electric current would. When a message is to be transferred, a neuron "fires," and its terminal buttons release chemicals called neurotransmitters (biochemical substances such as norepinephrine and dopamine), which make jumping the synapse possible. When an electrical signal comes to the end of one neuron, the cell fires, secreting the proper neurotransmitter into the synapse. This chemical messenger then crosses from the presynaptic neuron (the brain cell sending the message) to the postsynaptic neuron (the brain cell receiving the message), where it binds itself to the appropriate chemical receptor and influences the behavior of this second neuron.

The brain contains at least one hundred billion synapses. Researchers speculate that there may be hundreds of different neurotransmitters, and many neurons respond to more than one neurotransmitter. It is in this complex brain environment that psychiatric drugs operate, usually by influencing the neurotransmitters in one of several different ways.

Once a neurotransmitter binds to the receptors in the postsynaptic neuron, processes are set in motion in that neuron, either exciting it to keep sending the message along or inhibiting it to stop the transmission of the message. After the impulse is passed from one neuron to another, the neurotransmitter falls off the receptor and back into the synapse. There it is either taken back up into the presynaptic neuron (a kind of neuron recycling), broken down by enzymes and discarded to spinal fluid surrounding the brain, or reattaches itself to the receptor, thus strengthening the original signal that was sent from the presynaptic neuron.

Psychiatric drugs can influence each of these activities. They appear to act on systems built into the brain to regulate the behaviors connected to eating, sleeping, sexual ac-

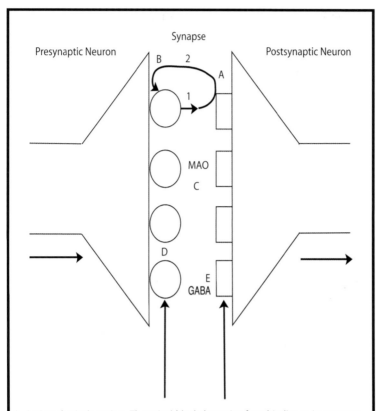

A. Antipsychotic drugs (e.g., Thorazine) block dopamine from binding to its receptor.

B. Many antidepressants (e.g., Tofranil, Elavil, Prozac) stop reuptake of neurotransmitters to the presynaptic cell, thus prolonging their life in the synapse. This increases neural flow.

C. MAO inhibitor antidepressants (e.g., Nardil, Parnate) inhibit MAO, thus prolonging the life of the neurotransmitters. This increases neural flow.

D. Amphetamines and cocaine cause increased release of some neurotransmitters from the synaptic neuron.

E. Some antianxiety drugs (e.g., Valium, Librium, Xanax) and sleeping pills (e.g., Dalmane, Halcion) increase the effectiveness of the neurotransmitter GABA at its receptor. This quiets the postsynaptic neural flow.

tivity, or other drives and rewards. Receptors and processes are developed to respond to internal chemical messages, and these external agents alter arousal, attention, emotional state, and thinking.

Gorman gives this explanation of how the specific type of psychiatric drugs used to treat schizophrenia (antipsychotics) work:

> The antipsychotic drugs—drugs that treat psychotic symptoms like hallucinations and delusions primarily in people with schizophrenia—block the ability of the neurotransmitter dopamine to bind to the dopamine receptor. Therefore, when a nerve signal reaches the end of a neuron that uses dopamine as its neurotransmitter, the pre-

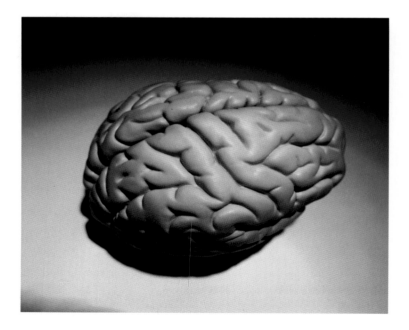

*Researchers are only just beginning to understand how the human brain functions.*

synaptic neuron secretes dopamine into the synapse, but the "keyhole"—the receptor—is blocked by the antipsychotic drug. The dopamine is then degraded by enzymes and some is taken back up into the presynaptic neuron, but it never gets to do its job, and so the neural signal cannot keep traveling from neuron to neuron to neuron. Examples of this kind of drug are Thorazine, Haldol, Prolixin, and Mellaril.

The newer antipsychotic drugs that have been developed, called atypical antipsychotics (such as clozapine, risperidone, and olanzapine), work in similar ways, except that they block less of the neurotransmitter dopamine. They also block another important neurotransmitter called serotonin.

## SUMMARY

The human brain has fascinated observers for centuries, but only in the last few decades have researchers had the tools to actually begin to understand how it functions. With understanding has come the increased ability to develop drugs that treat brain disorders such as schizophrenia.

*Today's treatments for schizophrenia are based on years of careful research.*

# 5 | Treatment Description

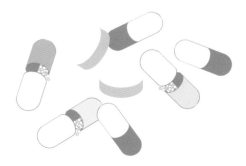

A compelling story of overcoming schizophrenia is the story of Frederick Frese, recorded in the June 1997 newsletter of www.schizophrenia.com. "Thirty years ago," the story begins, "he was locked up in an Ohio mental hospital, dazed and delusional, with paranoid schizophrenia. Twelve years later, he had become the chief psychologist for the very mental hospital system that had confined him."

Frese lets others know that schizophrenia does not have to be the end of life, and has become an example of a person who lives successfully with this disease. He now speaks around the country and is part of a national effort to end discrimination against people with mental illness.

He first experienced a breakdown at the age of twenty-five, when he was a Marine Corps captain. His job was to guard atomic weapons in Jacksonville, Florida, and he became convinced that enemy nations had hypnotized American leaders as part of a plot to take over the United States atomic weapons supply. Frese was hospitalized at a naval hospital in Bethesda, Maryland, and then discharged five months later, without any real understanding of what kind of disorder he had and how it should be treated.

A year later, Frese experienced his second breakdown. He was in a church in Milwaukee, where he "pictured himself changing from a man to monkey, then dog, snake, fish, and finally, an atom." He was delusional to the point of seeing himself on the inside of an atom bomb being loaded for use, and believed he was "the instrument to usher in Armageddon." Frese spent a few weeks in the hospital after that, but was then released to wander the streets for a year.

Eventually, Frese was declared insane by the State of Ohio, and after a forced stay in a maximum-security mental hospital cell, he was transferred to a Veterans Administration hospital. There, at last, he began to find real help when the doctors put him on a medicine that started to control his delusions.

Although he was hospitalized ten more times, Frese still managed to hold jobs; he earned a degree in international business management, and both a master's degree and doctorate in psychology. Amazingly, he then served for fifteen years as director of psychology at Western Reserve Psychiatric Hospital in Sagamore Hills, Ohio, where he had once been a patient. Frese also went on to marry his wife, Penny, and together they have three children. Regarding his schizophrenia, Frese comments, "These are times of change for us. . . . As I often say, in my thirty years with schizophrenia, there's never been a better time to be a person with serious mental illness. There's more hope than ever before."

## DIAGNOSIS

A correct diagnosis is always the first step in treating any mental disorder, and schizophrenia is no exception. How-

*This picture created by a patient in a psychiatric hospital illustrates the frightening world of schizophrenia.*

---

### Dangerous Delusion

In 1981, John Hinckley tried to assassinate President Ronald Reagan. Hinckley was diagnosed as schizophrenic, and part of his defense was that the assassination attempt was in response to his delusion that his action could help him win the affections of actress Jodie Foster. Psychiatrists for the defense and the prosecution disagreed vehemently on whether or not this type of thinking was really a delusion.

Even in the light of such spectacular cases as Hinckley's, however, it is important to remember that few patients with schizophrenia pose a danger to other people. Instead, they are more likely to become victims themselves.

---

ever, schizophrenia-like symptoms can be produced by many conditions, complicating the problem of diagnosis. Diseases whose symptoms mimic those of schizophrenia include temporal lobe *epilepsy*, brain tumors, *porphyria*, *syphilis* of the brain, and *trypanosomiasis*. Even pellagra, a nutritional deficiency, can produce similar symptoms.

Torrey gives the following example of another disease being mistaken for schizophrenia:

> Ruth was an 18-year-old Navy nursing aide. Following a flu-like illness, she developed headaches, began hearing voices talking to her, had feelings of unreality and loss of body boundaries, and became depressed. She slashed her wrists on instruction from the voices and was hospitalized. Her emotions were noted to be inappropriate, and she had mild disorders in her thinking. She was alternately treated as a depressive reaction and as a schizophrenic, although neurologists were also asked to see her because of the continuing headaches. She improved slowly over a three-month period and was discharged to be followed as an outpatient. Three months after dis-

**GLOSSARY**

*epilepsy:* A medical condition characterized by a disturbance of the electrical rhythms of the central nervous system. Often results in convulsions.

*porphyria:* A metabolic disorder accompanied by abdominal pain, peripheral neuropathy, and a variety of mental symptoms.

charge she died suddenly and without warning during an all-night prayer service. Autopsy revealed a viral infection of the brain which appeared to have been present for several months.

Because of such cases, Torrey writes that it is mandatory for all individuals first showing symptoms of schizophrenia to have a complete physical examination (including a neurological exam), with a thorough history taken, and standard laboratory tests done. In this way, other diseases that may be masquerading as schizophrenia can be diagnosed.

## AFTER THE DIAGNOSIS

Once other causes for psychotic behavior have been ruled out by a competent and experienced medical professional,

*Self-portraits created by a patient in a psychiatric hospital reveal the individual's confusion and distorted perceptions of self.*

*Drawings created by a patient with schizophrenia portray the bizarre reality this individual perceives.*

and schizophrenia has been diagnosed, decisions about treatment must be made.

In the case of many other mental disorders, doctors disagree on whether or not psychiatric drugs should be used. When it comes to schizophrenia, however, there is little debate. "Drugs are the most important treatment for schizophrenia, just as they are the most important treatment for many physical diseases of the human body," writes Torrey. "Drugs do not *cure,* but rather *control,* the symptoms of schizophrenia—as they do those of diabetes." This does not mean that doctors advocate using drugs alone to treat this disease, but they are seen as a necessary component of treatment. Along with antipsychotic drugs, additional therapies have proven effective. (See chapter eight.)

The use of antipsychotic drugs reduces the symptoms of schizophrenia, shortens stays in the hospital from the old average of several weeks or months, to days, and even lowers the chances that patients will have to be rehospitalized.

*Some psychiatric disorders can be treated with psychotherapy and no medication, but most practitioners today agree that "talk therapy" alone is not enough to effectively treat schizophrenia.*

John Davis reviewed twenty-four scientifically controlled studies testing the effectiveness of antipsychotic drugs. He concluded that all of the studies showed that patients given antipsychotic drugs are less likely to need to return to the hospital. "On the average, a person who takes the drugs has a 3-out-of-5 chance (60 percent) of not being rehospitalized, whereas the person who does not take the drugs has only a 1-out-of-5 chance (20 percent) of not being rehospitalized."

Antipsychotic drugs do not work equally well on all of the symptoms of schizophrenia. They are most effective in reducing the positive symptoms, such as delusions, hallucinations, aggressive or bizarre behavior, and thinking disorders. Antipsychotic drugs are not nearly so effective at treating the negative symptoms, such as apathy, ambivalence, and flat affect, and sometimes do not affect that class of symptoms at all. These drugs do not work equally well in all people with schizophrenia, either, although they can help reduce symptoms in 80 to 90 percent of those who take them.

The FDA bases its approval on specific research results. Sometimes, a particular use for a drug may have been thoroughly researched by many studies, while other uses lack the same amount of research. In that case, the drug label will only include the uses that have met the FDA's stringent research requirements. Physicians, however, may continue to prescribe that drug for other "off-label" uses.

## SIDE EFFECTS

As with all psychiatric drugs, antipsychotic drugs must be taken as directed in order to be effective. But many patients fail to comply with the treatment plan they are given. Even with all the positive effects of antipsychotic drugs, there is a negative side to drug treatment also.

In some cases, the same antipsychotic drugs that can lessen or alleviate positive symptoms seem to almost produce a "zombielike appearance," according Gorman. "Such patients," he writes, "may not be actively psychotic but they are not well either, often losing their motivation to do things and becoming comfortable sitting in one place for hours. The side effects of some of the antipsychotic drugs can mimic the 'negative' symptoms of schizophrenia." (See chapter seven.)

## TYPICAL OR ATYPICAL ANTIPSYCHOTIC DRUGS

Antipsychotic drugs are divided into two classes: typical and atypical. The older, typical antipsychotic drugs were first used in the late 1950s. For treatment and for the purpose of tracking side effects, these drugs are divided into high potency and low potency.

The typical antipsychotics work by strongly blocking the neurotransmitter dopamine and are most effective in treating the positive symptoms of schizophrenia. They are associated with a number of possible risks and side effects, so much so that it is sometimes difficult for patients to keep taking these medications. The rate of **noncompliance** among patients for whom typical antipsychotic drugs are prescribed is estimated to be as high as 40 percent. Because antipsychotic drugs have proven to be important not only in

**GLOSSARY**

*noncompliance:* Not adhering to the treatment plan.

GLOSSARY

*relapse:* To slip or fall back into a former condition after showing improvement.

relieving symptoms of schizophrenia but are also thought to inhibit the progression of the illness, it is vital that patients adhere to their treatment with psychiatric drugs. High rates of noncompliance can also lead to higher rates of *relapse*.

## TYPICAL ANTIPSYCHOTICS

### High-Potency Typical Antipsychotics

- haloperidol (Haldol)
- fluphenazine HCl (Prolixin)
- trifluoperazine HCl (Stelazine)
- thiothixene HCl (Navane)

### Low-Potency Typical Antipsychotics

- chlorpromazine (Thorazine)
- thioridazine (Mellaril)

### Midway Between Low and High Potency

- perphenazine (Trilafon)

## ATYPICAL ANTIPSYCHOTICS

The high incidence of side effects with the typical antipsychotic drugs spurred researchers to find medications that could treat serious illnesses such as schizophrenia without so many negative results. Specifically, the atypical antipsychotics are less likely to cause extrapyramidal symptoms (EPS), they are more effective in treating schizophrenia that

*Prescription medications offer hope to those who suffer from schizophrenia.*

### Who can diagnose a psychiatric disorder?

- psychiatrists
- psychiatric advanced practice nurses
- medical doctors
- clinical nurse specialists
- nurse psychiatrists
- social workers
- psychologists

However, in most of the United States only medical doctors, psychiatrists, clinical nurse specialists, nurse psychiatrists, and advanced practice nurses can prescribe psychotropic medication.

has not responded to other drugs, and they are more likely to relieve the negative symptoms of the disease. The atypicals work by blocking dopamine, though not as strongly as the typical antipsychotics, and by also blocking serotonin. At one time, the "dopamine hypothesis" of schizophrenia seemed to explain the causes of the disease. Because of the way the atypical antipsychotics, operate, however, the hypothesis is now in question.

The first of the atypical antipsychotics, clozapine (Clozaril), was introduced in 1990 in the United States. This medication was actually a very old medication, having been used in other countries prior to its approval in the United States. Risperidone (Risperdal) was released in 1994. Since

then, three other atypical antipsychotics have been approved by the U.S. Food and Drug Administration.

Atypical antipsychotics include:

- clozapine (Clozaril)
- risperidone (Risperdal)
- olanzapine (Zyprexa)
- quetiapine fumerate (Seroquel)
- ziprasidone HCl (Geodon)

Three more atypical antipsychotics are currently being
developed:

- iloperidone
- amisulpride
- aripiprazole

## PLANS FOR TREATMENT OF SCHIZOPHRENIA

Schizophrenia is a disease that can present in many different ways and can follow many different courses. Treatment
must be tailored to these variables. In *The New Psychiatry*,
Gorman suggests the following treatment approaches for
five common situations involving people with schizophrenia:

I. An acutely psychotic patient is brought to the emergency room.

1. Take medical and psychiatric history. Perform
physical and do blood tests.
2. With permission from the patient, give one dose of
a high-potency antipsychotic drug (Haldol or Prolixin are common choices).

*Electric shock therapy was once a common treatment for patients with schizophrenia. Today, it is still used under controlled circumstances, but medications are usually the first-choice treatment.*

3. Wait a while, with the patient in a safe place, to see if the patient becomes calm. (If the patient remains agitated or shows a continuing potential for violence, many psychiatrists recommend repeated doses of lorazepam (Ativan), a benzodiazepine drug, either by mouth or by injection.

4. After the patient becomes calm, he may need to be admitted to the hospital. He can then be started on an antipsychotic medicine, such as risperidone (Risperdal). The beginning dose is one milligram twice a day, with a graduated increase to three milligrams twice a day. Dosing depends on many things, including the age of the patient. Most prac-

titioners start at the lowest dose possible to make
sure the patient can tolerate the medication before
the dose is increased.

II. For a patient with schizophrenia whose situation is
not an emergency, begin an antipsychotic medicine
such as risperidone and try to get the patient's family involved in family therapy. The patient herself
should also begin rehabilitative therapies, such as
those designed to help with social skills.

III. In the case of a patient with schizophrenia who re-
fuses treatment, determine if this refusal is due to
the side effects of the drugs. If so, it may be possible to change to a medication that does not produce
the side effect that the patient dislikes.

IV. If the patient does not respond to different typical
antipsychotic drugs, the psychiatrist can add a
mood-stabilizing dug, such as lithium or Depakote,
or switch to the atypical antipsychotic drug clozapine (Clozaril). *Electroconvulsive* therapy may also
be tried.

> **GLOSSARY**
>
> *electroconvul-
> sive: A treatment
> in which elec-
> trodes introduce
> electrical charges
> to particular parts
> of the brain.*

V. When the patient with schizophrenia has mainly
negative symptoms, determine the source of the
problems. If it is post-psychotic depression, the patient can be started on an antidepressant medication, such as imipramine (Tofranil). The patient
may be switched to an atypical antipsychotic drug
that may be better at dealing with negative symptoms. There are two of these drugs available,
risperidone (Risperdal) and clozapine (Clozaril).
   A dopamine-enhancing drug such as Mazindol
can be added to the traditional antipsychotic drug,

but this should only be done under the supervision of a knowledgeable psychopharmacologist.

## PATIENTS WHO REFUSE TREATMENT

It is not unusual for patients with schizophrenia to refuse treatment. Sometimes, the reason for this may be the desire to avoid the unpleasant side effects of the antipsychotic medication, which many patients find hard to tolerate. At other times, the delusions the patient experiences keep her from accepting treatment. For instance, she may hear voices that tell her not to take her medicines. Or she may feel she is cured and stop taking the medicine.

Although the patient usually has the right to refuse treatment, it is still the doctor's responsibility to try to convince her to take the medicine, just as he would attempt to convince someone with a serious physical illness to take medication that could help.

It the psychiatrist's efforts to convince her fail, then by legal and ethical standards, he must determine if her refusal to take her medication might lead to a tragedy. Gorman puts it this way: "Rather than allow a psychotic patient to jump in front of a car or attack someone, it seems reasonable to administer an antipsychotic drug that may clear up the hallucinations and delusions responsible for the patient's violent potential. It does not seem right to permit someone in the clutches of psychosis to end his life; the patient has the right to make that decision with a clear mind, free of psychotic interference." He adds that the question of whether or not to force someone to take medication is now one of the most controversial areas of psychiatry, especially considering possible legal ramifications.

In most states, a psychotic patient who presents a clear, immediate threat to herself or others can be hospitalized involuntarily. Once there, however, it usually takes another court order to administer drugs against her will. "It is often the case," writes Gorman, "that the judge decides it is too dangerous to grant the patient's wish to be released from the hospital but grants the patient's decision to refuse medication."

This can mean a long period of hospitalization, because for patients who have schizophrenia, there is not much chance that they will recover without psychiatric medications. Persuasion on the part of the patient's family is often the best, and only other recourse to get the patient to cooperate with her treatment plan.

## SUMMARY

Correct diagnosis and prompt treatment with the appropriate psychiatric medication is usually the patient's best hope to combat schizophrenia. Such care has been shown to lead to a more favorable prognosis for the patient's future.

*The expressions of a person with schizophrenia may appear strange and inappropriate to the situation.*

# 6 | Case Studies

Each individual who experiences schizophrenia is unique. But many people with schizophrenia have some things in common. Drug therapy will help most of them handle their symptoms. For many, it will make possible a more normal and satisfying life.

## A FAMOUS SCHIZOPHRENIA CASE STUDY

Possible causes of schizophrenia have been debated for decades. One family gives researchers a strong indication that the disease may have a genetic basis.

In the 1930s, four genetically identical quadruplets—girls—were born to a family that researchers would eventually rename the Genains, from the Greek words that mean "dreadful gene," in order to protect their privacy. The girls would also be assigned fictional first names based on the initials of the National Institute of Mental Health (NIMH) in

---

### Neurotransmitters and Mental Disorders

---

| Neurotransmitter | Related Mental Disorders |
|---|---|
| dopamine | schizophrenia; drug addiction |
| norepinephrine | mood disorders; anxiety disorders |
| beta-endorphin | drug addiction |
| serotonin | mood disorders |
| gamma-aminobutyric acid | anxiety disorders |

From *Exploring Abnormal Psychology*, by Perrotto and Culkin.

---

Washington, D.C., where their case would be studied. These names were Nora, Iris, Myra, and Hester.

During their childhood, the Genain sisters each exhibited emotional and behavioral disturbances. When they were admitted to NIMH while in their early twenties, the quadruplets were diagnosed as having schizophrenia. They stayed at NIMH for three years, during which time they were tested and treated with the most up-to-date techniques.

In 1981, NIMH again tested the Genain sisters with modern technology that had not been available during their first visit. The neuropsychological testing, brain imaging, and biochemical evaluations of the sisters provided material for many in-depth studies of schizophrenia. On their first visit to NIMH, the sisters showed a variety of symptoms. Nora was withdrawn, hallucinating, delusional, and slow of speech. Iris complained of numerous physical symptoms, insomnia, a belief that she was being watched, and auditory hallucinations. Myra, the least impaired, showed psychomotor slowness, overly dramatic behavior, anxiety, and depression. Hester had the most severe problems; she was fearful, confused, withdrawn, and hallucinating.

In the years between their first and second stay at NIMH, Nora, Iris, and Hester stayed several times at state mental hospitals. Originally, the sisters had been diagnosed with schizophrenic reaction, catatonic type. In the years between NIMH admissions, they were also diagnosed with disorganized schizophrenia and chronic undifferentiated schizophrenia. During these years, Nora and Iris were admitted for psychiatric treatment six times. They had attempted—and failed—at several jobs, and they spent a great

*The Genain sisters helped researchers piece together a little more of schizophrenia's puzzle.*

*Some people with schizophrenia suffer from paranoia. They may believe that there are eyes constantly watching them.*

deal of their time in group or foster care homes. Hester, the sister who had the most severe problems, was admitted for treatment twelve times. Myra was the healthiest of the quadruplets, with no hospital admissions other than those at NIMH. She married, worked, and raised two children in these years. During their second stay at NIMH, in 1981, Nora and Iris were diagnosed as chronic undifferentiated schizophrenics. Myra and Hester were given the diagnosis of schizophrenia, residual type.

It is believed by researchers that the quadruplets' apparent genetic predisposition to schizophrenia came from their father, who exhibited paranoid thinking and severe emotional disturbances. "He was erratic, suspicious, domineering, and prone to excessive drinking," wrote the researchers. His mother (the sisters' grandmother) had once been hospitalized for a nervous breakdown, and other relatives on his side of the family also showed signs of psychological problems.

None of the four Genain sisters showed clear structural abnormalities in their brains (such as the enlarged *ventricles* that appear in 25 to 50 percent of patients with schizophrenia), which may result from both genetic and environmental factors. However, all four showed "deficits in frontal lobe electrical and chemical activity" and "the visual regions of their brains showed unusual activity that might have indicated perceptual disturbances or hallucinations. Nora and Hester had more evidence of brain dysfunction than Myra and Iris.

Researchers studied the influences of their family on the Genain sisters and found that these influences were damaging. Their father had been suspicious and invasive; he was prone to fits of frenzy and rage. In addition, their father was emotionally and perhaps even sexually abusive toward them. Their mother had been overprotective and restrictive. The sisters were not permitted to play with other

> **GLOSSARY**
>
> **ventricles:** *Any of the communicating cavities in the brain that are continuous with the central canal of the spinal cord.*

children; later, they were not permitted to date. Their parents actively promoted jealousy and competition among the girls and even assigned them ranks in the family, playing them off against one another.

## CASES THAT RESEMBLE SCHIZOPHRENIA

Other kinds of mental illness display symptoms similar to those of schizophrenia. In some cases, the difference is a matter of duration.

### *Brief Reactive Psychosis*

When Perry took a job distributing emergency food supplies in the Sudan, he and his coworker spent weeks at a time in isolated villages where they could neither speak nor understand the native language. At times, when there were interruptions in the transfer of supplies and Perry and his coworker temporarily ran out of food to distribute, Perry witnessed the despair and sometimes the anger of the starving people he had come to help.

After three months on the job, Perry's coworker walked into the tiny hut the men shared and found Perry huddled on the floor with a sleeping mat covering his entire body and head, trying to hide from the "natives who were coming to kill him." By the time his coworker could arrange for transport to a hospital, Perry acted very much like a person diagnosed with schizophrenia.

However, after two weeks of drug therapy at the hospital, Perry was completely well. He was diagnosed with brief reactive psychosis, but if his illness had lasted longer than two weeks and up to six months, it would have been diagnosed as a schizophreniform disorder.

*Other kinds of mental disorders may resemble schizophrenia. Schizophrenia, however, lasts longer than a brief episode.*

At times, when otherwise normal individuals experience overwhelming stress (soldiers under enemy fire, people held in concentration camps), extreme sensory deprivation (someone alone in a lifeboat on the ocean for an extended period of time), or a short viral infection of the brain (encephalitis and other diseases), they may have brief episodes that mimic schizophrenia. In such cases hallucinations and delusions are the most common symptoms. Thinking disorders are much less common.

### *Postpartum Schizophrenic-Like Symptoms*

When Angela gave birth to her second child, a son, the family was delighted. Even little Jessica, five years old, was excited about having a new brother.

About four days after Angela brought baby Colin home from the hospital, however, strange things started happening. Angela suddenly wanted nothing to do with Colin. When her husband came home from work, he found the new baby wailing with hunger in his crib and Jessica hiding in her room, whimpering that mommy was talking "crazy."

When he confronted her, Angela admitted to her husband that she was afraid to go near Colin, since she kept hearing voices that told her to strangle the infant.

When Angela was admitted to the hospital and treated with psychiatric drugs, however, her symptoms went away within two weeks and never returned.

Although ***postpartum*** depression is a fairly common occurrence, usually attributable to changes in hormone levels and various other stressors, schizophrenic-like symptoms develop in the new mother in about one in a thousand births.

In these cases, the new mother may experience delusions, such as believing that her baby is terminally ill or handicapped in some way. Or she may hallucinate, hearing voices that instruct her to harm or even murder the child. A very small number of these cases go on to become a true schizophrenic disorder. In most cases, however, medications usually help quickly, resolving the problem within just a few weeks.

## SUMMARY

Schizophrenia can present in many different ways and can follow various courses. Added to this difficulty is the fact that so many other mental disorders, and even some physical disorders, can produce symptoms that mimic those of schizophrenia. Long-term studies such as those done on the Genain sisters provide valuable information for medical professionals who treat this disease, as well as for researchers who work to create more effective medications with fewer side effects.

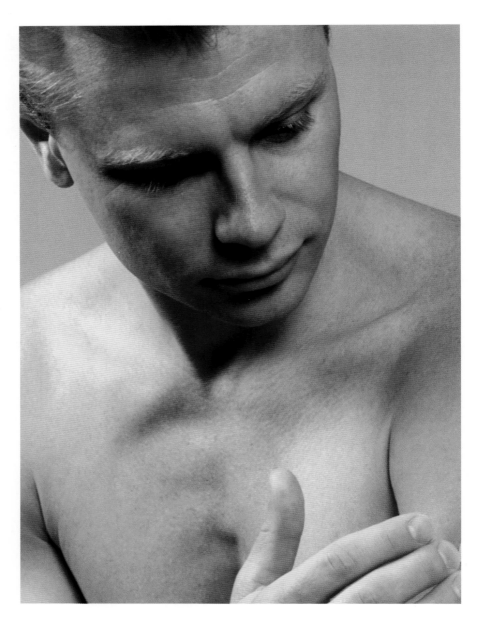

*Psychiatric drugs affect the entire body—not just the brain—and this means they may cause side effects that range from annoying to dangerous. Anyone taking a psychiatric drug should pay attention to any changes he notices (including something as simple as a skin rash) and report them immediately to his doctor or other healthcare practitioner.*

# 7 | Risks and Side Effects

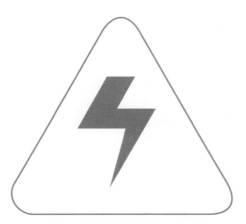

In the January 1997 issue of the newsletter at www.schizophrenia.com, Pamela Spiro Wagner wrote an account of her experiences with several of the antipsychotic medications used to treat schizophrenia.

Wagner calls these medications a "distinctly mixed blessing," and details some of the side effects she experienced while taking them. She was on fluphenazine (Prolixin) for years, but the treatment was not totally successful, since she still had to be admitted to the hospital one or two times per year. Wagner says she "hated the stuff, refused to take it on my own," and so was given long-acting injections of the drug.

When clozapine (Clozaril), which was touted as a "wonder drug," was approved, her doctors promptly tried the new medication with her. Wagner experienced little change at first and was discharged from the hospital with enough pills for a week. However, after she reached therapeutic levels of the drug, she recounts that "all hell broke loose," and she felt she experienced "every side effect in the book and then some."

Her side effects included profound sedation, causing her to sleep as much as sixteen hours out of twenty-four. She experienced drooling, and within a short time of taking her medication, she found herself unable to swallow her saliva. When she complained of these problems, she was ignored for the most part, because her doctor did not feel they fit in with the profile of the drug's expected side effects.

Wagner eventually returned to taking Prolixin injections, for lack of a better treatment. She tried risperidone (Risperdal), but had such a serious reaction she had to be hospitalized. She had all but decided that she would never find a medication that would help her without doing significant harm. Then her therapist told her about olanzapine (Zyprexa).

She experienced almost no negative side effects on olanzapine. Instead, Wagner saw the negative symptoms that had seemed a permanent part of her life for years begin to change. She writes, that "one night, not long after starting the new drug, I took a bath, not because someone suggested I needed it, but because it suddenly seemed to me that I'd feel better if my body were clean. The next day, I 'decided' my kitchen was messy . . . and put on the radio and got to work—doing the dishes voluntarily and without help for literally the first time in years, even scrubbing the floor on my hands and knees."

Wagner, who had not been able to listen to radio programs for years because she had been convinced that messages were being sent specifically to her through these programs, now turned on the radio and enjoyed listening. Soon, she stopped needing constant "white noise" to drown out the voices she had heard previously—voices that had now grown so quiet she could barely hear them.

*Psychiatric drugs can provide relief from the disturbing voices sometimes caused by schizophrenia.*

*Tardive dyskinesia is a possible side effect of antipsychotic medications. It includes bizarre and involuntary facial movements.*

Wagner saw numerous changes as a result of taking olanzapine. The most astounding, according to her, was that for the first time in years she wore regular pajamas to bed instead of going to sleep in her street clothes and shoes.

Although Wagner continues to experience some sleepiness on the drug, and she has also had a "substantial weight gain," she writes that these are "minor glitches in a medication regimen that by and large has been . . . something very nearly miraculous."

## SIDE EFFECTS OF TYPICAL ANTIPSYCHOTICS

This is not an exhaustive list of possible side effects, but it does contain the most prominent symptoms.

### Sedation

Low-potency typical antipsychotic drugs, such as chlorpromazine (Thorazine), and thioridazine (Mellaril) are more likely to sedate patients.

### Tardive Dyskinesia

Tardive dyskinesia is a movement disorder induced by antipsychotic drugs. It is characterized by involuntary facial movements, such as grimacing, lip-smacking, and chewing motions. Although less common, it may also involve involuntary arm movements or rocking back and forth. Antipsychotic drugs must usually be taken for years to produce this side effect, but in the case of elderly patients and some younger ones as well, signs of tardive dsykinesia may begin after just a few months. Stopping the antipsychotic drug may bring an end to tardive dsykinesia, but this means that the patient may become psychotic again. In some patients, tardive dyskinesia becomes a permanent problem, even after the antipsychotic drug is stopped.

### Extrapyramidal Symptoms

Some of the typical antipsychotics, particularly the ones classified as high-potency (haloperidol [Haldol], fluphenazine [Prolixin], thiothixene [Navane], and trifluoperazine [Stelazine]), can cause side effects that have to do with the extrapyramidal motor system. This body system helps control movement; the neurological side effects of high-potency typical antipsychotics are known as extrapyramidal symptoms (EPS).

### Parkinsonian-Like Effects
### (resembles symptoms of Parkinson's disease)

- tremor
- muscle rigidity
- slowing of movement
- sad facial expression (regardless of the patient's mood)

### GLOSSARY

**basal ganglia:** *Four masses of gray matter located deep in the cerebral hemispheres. Chemical substances that affect basal ganglionic function are acetylcholine, dopamine, gamma-aminobutyric acid (GABA) and serotonin.*

The *basal ganglia* is a major part of the extrapyramidal motor system, and it is thought that these side effects are caused when dopamine is blocked there. There are medications available to reverse these side effects, but they do not always work.

### Dystonias

These are sudden muscle stiffening that may cause a sudden contraction in the arms, neck, or face. Medications are available to reverse this side effect.

### Akathisia

This is a feeling of jumpiness, described as "my legs are restless," "I feel like I'm jumping out of my skin," "I just can't sit still." Medications can treat this side effect.

*A person experiencing Parkinsonian-like side effects from taking an antipsychotic drug may constantly have a sad expression, regardless of his actual mood.*

*Weight gain is one side effect of taking some antipsychotic medications. This can be particularly disturbing to those who have always emphasized physical fitness in their lives. As many as half of all patients taking a typical antipsychotic are obese—but when a person's schizophrenia is severe, weight gain is preferable to living without the medication.*

### *Other Side Effects*

- weight gain. With ongoing use of these antipsychotics, a patient may gain fifteen to seventy-five pounds, probably because of neurotransmitter dysregulation. The present estimate is that 35 to 50 percent of treated patients are obese.
- risk of seizure
- neuroleptic malignant syndrome (includes high fever and decreased consciousness)

## SIDE EFFECTS OF ATYPICAL ANTIPSYCHOTICS

The atypical antipsychotics include clozapine (Clozaril), risperidone (Risperdal), olanzapine (Zyprexa), quetiapine fumerate (Seroquel), and ziprasidone (Geodon). Although researchers know that the atypical antispychotics do a good job of treating the symptoms of schizophrenia with fewer side effects, they are not completely sure why this is the case. While these drugs are not as effective in blocking dopamine, they also block the binding of serotonin.

While clozapine is not as likely as the typical antipsychotics to cause tardive dyskinesia or affect the part of the motor system that helps control movement, it can cause a potentially fatal blood disorder called agranulocytosis in about one percent of those who take it. In agranulocytosis, the bone marrow stops making a type of white blood cell, which can lead to infection. The drug must be stopped immediately when this condition is discovered or the patient can die from infection. Patients who take clozapine need to have weekly blood tests to monitor their white blood cell count. Clozapine also increases the risk of having *seizures* and of gaining weight, and can lead to uncontrollable salivation.

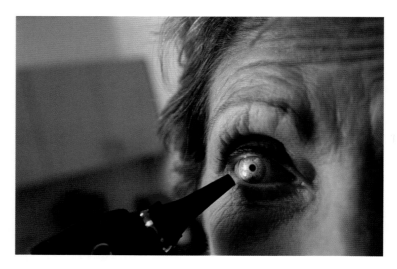

*Some forms of antipsychotic drugs may cause cataracts and changes in the eye's lens. Patients taking these drugs should have regular eye exams.*

Risperidone and olanzapine are not considered as likely to cause EPS as the typical antipsychotics (although there needs to be more years of observing its effects to be absolutely sure), and do not produce agranulocytosis. All the facts are not yet in regarding the likelihood of whether or not this drug will cause tardive dyskinesia.

There have been questions about quetiapine fumerate and the formation of ***cataracts***, and lens changes have been noted in patients who take the drug for a long time. It is currently recommended that patients have ophthalmologic exams before taking quetiapine, and every six months while they take it.

Ziprasidone is the most likely of the atypical antipsychotic medications to lead to a specific type of heart ***dysrhythmia*** that can cause sudden death. Electrocardiograms are done routinely to monitor any changes that might lead to dysrhythmias.

**GLOSSARY**

**cataracts:** *An eye disease in which the clear lens becomes opaque, resulting in partial or total blindness.*

**dysrhythmia:** *An abnormal rhythm.*

## SUMMARY

All medications have side effects. Some are slight and make very little difference to the patient. Other side effects are so serious as to be debilitating, and patients may even stop their treatment because of these effects.

Knowing the possible side effects before the treatment begins can sometimes be a help to patients. If there are other medications available to lessen the side effects, this information also must be provided to the patient.

*Marijuana can worsen schizophrenia's symptoms.*

# 8 | Alternative and Supplementary Treatments

In many cases, mental disorders can be effectively treated with therapy or drugs, or with a combination of both. For patients with schizophrenia, treatment with psychiatric drugs is essential, but therapy and other factors may also help these patients function more effectively and live a richer, fuller life.

## AVOIDING "RECREATIONAL" DRUGS

Alcohol and drug abuse is common among people with schizophrenia, but these people are more likely to have a particularly severe reaction to these drugs. Amphetamines, cocaine, PCP, and marijuana can cause the symptoms of schizophrenia to worsen in some individuals with this disorder.

Nicotine is used by many people with schizophrenia, and is in fact the most common form of substance abuse in

*Research indicates that smoking interferes with a patient's response to antipsychotic medications.*

these patients. It is believed that three times as many people with schizophrenia smoke as do people in the general population. However, smoking has been shown to interfere with patients' response to antipsychotic drugs, and patients who smoke may actually need to take higher doses of these drugs in order to achieve the same affect. This can be a serious problem, since higher doses can cause more side effects.

## THERAPY

### *Psychodynamic Therapy*

At one time, psychodynamic therapy was the main type of therapy used in treating those with schizophrenia. Many therapists, including Freud, doubted the effectiveness of this type of therapy with psychotic patients, however.

Research has now shown that insight-oriented psychotherapy alone may even be harmful in some cases be-

---

### When Psychiatric Medicines May Be Needed

When a patient exhibits:

- suicidal thoughts
- presence of hallucinations or delusions
- decrease in ability to function (includes inability to sleep, eat, work, care for children, perform personal hygiene)
- self-destructive behavior
- uncontrollable compulsions (constant washing or checking)

---

## When Either Psychiatric Medicines or Psychotherapy May Work (depending on the severity of the condition)

When a patient exhibits:

- depression that does not include suicidal thoughts, loss of function, or inability to eat or sleep
- generalized anxiety disorder
- social phobia
- bulimia

---

cause "probing interpretations may overstimulate and distress the patient." Torrey described using this type of therapy with patients who have schizophrenia as being "analogous to directing a flood into a town already ravaged by a tornado."

### Supportive Psychotherapy

This psychotherapy uses practical advice, concrete problem-solving, and empathic understanding to provide support for people with schizophrenia, and it has been found to provide a modest amount of benefit to patients. The best results occur when psychotherapy is used together with antipsychotic medications and when the therapy deals with the patient's social withdrawal, maladaptive behaviors, and the practical problems he faces in his everyday life.

### Family Therapy

While it is clear that families do not cause schizophrenia, families can be educated about how to care for and be

*Families need to be involved in loved ones' treatments.*

supportive of a member with this disease. In many cases, schizophrenia means that the patient will need to live with his family for his entire life. Family members can experience great stress and emotional pain when they must watch someone they love deal with schizophrenia. Family therapy can help these family members deal with their feelings. It can also provide understanding and insight into the nature and treatment of schizophrenia, and teach them how to monitor the illness and how to provide a helpful, low-stress environment for the patient. Gerard Hogarty, a social worker, has provided evidence that medication plus family therapy can actually decrease the likelihood of a relapse, as compared to treatment with medication alone.

### Rehabilitative Therapy

Rehabilitative therapy is designed to teach patients how to establish relationships and learn social skills. Employ-

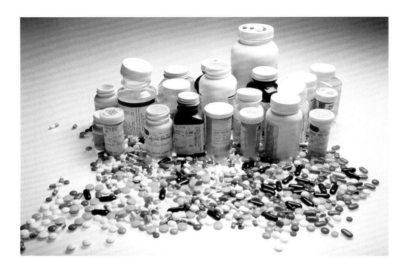

*Psychiatric drugs play a major role in the treatment of schizo-phrenia—but other therapies can also contribute to the individual's well-being.*

ment programs may also be part of rehabilitative therapy. Because patients with schizophrenia frequently have difficulty finding and keeping jobs, training in the skills necessary to be employed is an important part of this therapy.

## SUMMARY

Although medical professionals agree that antipsychotic medications are the most essential component in a treatment plan for patients with schizophrenia, other components, such as the various therapies available, can also contribute to a patient's care and well-being.

# FURTHER READING

Bellack, Alan S., Kim T. Mueser, Susan Gingerich, and Julie Agresta. *Social Skills Training for Schizophrenia, A Step-by-Step Guide.* New York: The Guilford Press, 1997.

Bonder, Bette R. *Psychopathology & Function, Second Edition.* Thorofare, N.J.: Slack, 1995.

Copeland, Mary Ellen. *Winning Against Relapse.* New York: New Harbinger, 1998.

Drummond, Edward, M.D. *The Complete Guide to Psychiatric Drugs.* New York: John Wiley & Sons, 2000.

Gorman, Jack M. *The New Psychiatry.* New York: St. Martin's Press, 1996.

Gorman, Jack M. *The Essential Guide to Psychiatric Drugs.* New York: St. Martin's Griffin, 1997.

Perrotto, Richard S., and Joseph Culkin. *Exploring Abnormal Psychology.* New York: HarperCollins, 1993.

Sacks, Oliver. *An Anthropologist on Mars, Seven Paradoxical Tales.* New York: Alfred A. Knopf, 1995.

Torrey, E. Fuller. *Surviving Schizophrenia, A Family Manual.* New York: Harper & Row, 1983.

# FOR MORE INFORMATION

American Psychological Association
750 First Street, N.E.
Washington, DC 20002
www.apa.org

American Psychiatric Association
1400 K St., N.W.
Washington, DC 20005
www.psych.org

National Alliance for the Mentally Ill
200 North Glebe Road
Suite 1015
Arlington, VA 22203
800-950-NAMI

National Institute of Mental Health
Public Inquiries
5600 Fishers Lane
Room 7C-02
Rockville, MD 20857

National Mental Health Association
1021 Prince Street
Alexandria, VA 22314-2971
800-969-NMHA
www.nmha.org

The Schizophrenia Homepage
www.shizophrenia.com

Publisher's Note:
The Web sites listed on this page were active at the time of publication. The publisher is not responsible for Web sites that have changed their address or discontinued operation since the date of publication. The publisher will review and update the Web sites upon each reprint.

# INDEX

# BIOGRAPHIES

Shirley Brinkerhoff is a writer, editor, speaker, and musician. She graduated Summa Cum Laude from Cornerstone University with a Bachelor of Music degree, and from Western Michigan University with a Master of Music degree. She has published six young adult novels, eleven informational books for young people, scores of short stories and articles, and teaches at writers' conferences throughout the United States.

Mary Ann Johnson is a licensed child and adolescent clinical nurse specialist and a family psychiatric nurse practitioner in the state of Massachusetts. She completed her psychotherapy training at Cambridge Hospital and her psychopharmacology training at Massachusetts General Hospital. She is the director of clinical trials in the pediatric psychopharmacology research unit at Massachusetts General Hospital, and she also has her own private pracctice.

Donald Esherick has spent seventeen years working in the pharmaceutical industry and is currently an associate director of Worldwide Regulatory Affairs with Wyeth Research in Philadelphia, Pennsylvania. He specializes in the chemistry section (manufacture and testing) of investigational and marketed drugs.